The Rural Vision
France and America
in the Late Nineteenth Century

Proceedings of a symposium held at Joslyn Art Museum,
Omaha, Nebraska, November 6, 1982, in conjunction with the exhibition
Jules Breton and the French Rural Tradition

The Rural Vision
France and America
in the Late Nineteenth Century

Hollister Sturges, Editor

Joslyn Art Museum, Omaha, Nebraska
distributed by the University of Nebraska Press

This publication is funded in part by a grant from the
National Endowment for the Humanities.

Cover: Jules Breton, *The Weeders,* 1860. Joslyn Art Museum.
Design: Abigail Sturges
Typography: Bauer Typography
Production and Lithography: Eastern Press, Inc.

Library of Congress Cataloging-in-Publication Data
The Rural vision.

   "Proceedings of a symposium held at Joslyn Art Museum,
Omaha, Nebraska, November 6, 1982, in conjunction with the
exhibition Jules Breton and the French rural tradition"—
   Includes index.
   1. Country life in art—Congresses. 2. Breton, Jules, 1827-
1906—Themes, motives—Congresses. 3. Genre Painting—
French—Congresses. 4. Genre painting—19th century—
France—Congresses. 5. Genre painting, American—
Congresses. 6. Genre painting—19th Century-Congresses.
I. Sturges, Hollister. II. Joslyn Art Museum.

ISBN 0-936364-19-X

Contents

Preface

The papers in this volume were first delivered at a symposium organized in conjunction with the exhibition *Jules Breton and the French Rural Tradition* at the Joslyn Art Museum, Omaha, Nebraska. While rural life has been the subject of celebration and study since the Renaissance, Jules Breton's paintings of nineteenth-century French peasants raise a particularly interesting set of questions because of the dominance of his vision in his own day, his enduring popularity, and the values his works embody. Honored by the standards of his own age, including election to the prestigious Institute of France, Breton was an artist whose pictures were eagerly sought after by patrons in France, England, and especially America. If his reputation in the history of art has fluctuated, today his work continues to have strong appeal for a wide audience and deserves reevaluation.

During the Omaha exhibition, Breton's paintings and drawings provoked a myriad of positive responses, suggesting that the artist still has currency in the 1980s. Reaction centered on his capacity to project a convincing scene of earthy reality and, almost paradoxically, a nineteenth-century pastoral ideal. One exhibition visitor, a prosperous Omaha banker in his eighties, discussed nostalgically how Breton's pictures recalled memories of his boyhood in northern Europe. He particularly admired an oil sketch of a sow trussed up on a wheelbarrow. It was commonplace, he recounted, for a sow to be transported to a neighbor's to be mated with a boar and, after the boar had "had his way with her" and "bloodied her up a bit," the sow was carted home. A less experienced eye would have presumed the pig destined for the butcher, while those who know Breton only from his Salon pictures might be surprised at his unflinching depiction of country life.

Breton's second source of appeal is his vision of the nobility, wholesomeness, and beauty of rustic ways and of the social harmony of the agrarian community. Fertile plains, communal and solitary labor, moments of rest and repose, and country religious ceremonies constitute his portrait of French rural life. Above all, however, he projects his idealized vision through images of youthful peasant women. The world of Breton is a panorama of rural maidens working in the fields, resting in reflective solitude, or absorbed in such tasks as knitting. Through his realization of this ideal, this archetypal image of the rural maiden, Breton is able to personify the beauty, innocence, serenity, and virtue of the bucolic life. It is a potent ideal that has also found strong expression in literary fiction and film and continues to be one of the appealing fantasies of our modern urban culture.

To arrive at a better understanding of Breton and the rural values championed in his art, the Joslyn Art Museum invited scholars in diverse fields to present papers from the perspective of their discipline. While all participants focused on the depiction of rural life, the symposium was broadened to include papers on nineteenth- and early twentieth-century America as well as France, and photography and literature as well as painting. Because Nebraska, like France, has a formidable agricultural tradition of its own and celebrants to sing its praises, two of the discussions focused on Nebraska artists: photographer Soloman Butcher and novelist Willa Cather.

The papers in this volume explore the perceptions of

artists of disparate temperament, the values of their patrons and public, and the realities of two different kinds of rural experience: that of the traditional French peasant and that of the American settler. Social historian Robert J. Bezucha demonstrates how the urban values of the bourgeois public and the political forces of the Third Republic conditioned artistic representation of the countryside. My own paper examines the roots of Breton's elevated conception of the peasantry and compares it with that of Jean-François Millet. Gabriel P. Weisberg discusses the role of the popular Swiss painter, Léopold Robert, in Breton's artistic formation.

Examining visions of rural experience on this side of the Atlantic, Susan J. Rosowski establishes the connection between Willa Cather and French painters Breton and Millet, and shows how the Nebraska author pioneered an ennobled conception of rural life. Rosowski draws further parallels between Cather and the French painters, noting the creative tension the novelist maintains in balancing the opposing impulses toward the real and the ideal. In her discussion of late nineteenth-century American painting, Patricia Hills demonstrates that pictures of rural life do not illustrate farming of that period, but rather create images of a pre-industrial era. Such images, she advances, reveal the values of an urban entrepreneurial class, nostalgic for the myth of the American farmer of the frontier. Finally, John E. Carter contrasts the yeoman of America with the peasant of Europe and discusses one interpreter of the American dream, the documentary photographer of the Nebraska settlement, Solomon Butcher.

Central to all these discussions are the values and forces which condition the perceptions of the artists. By juxtaposing the cultures of France and America, and by looking at artists of different sensibility who also are working in different media, this collection of papers examines the variables that constitute the artistic representation of rural life. The vitality of this expression enriches not only our experience of Jules Breton, but illuminates our understanding of the continuing dialectic between urban and rural values.

For gracious assistance and support in the preparation of this publication, I wish to thank Henry Flood Robert, Jr., Director of the Joslyn Art Museum, who encouraged the project from its inception; Petra ten-Doesschate Chu, Professor of Art History at Seton Hall University, who carefully read all the manuscripts and contributed valuable suggestions to the authors; Janet L. Farber, Curatorial Assistant, European Art Department, Joslyn Art Museum, who proofread the manuscripts; and especially Ruby C. Hagerbaumer, Curatorial Assistant at Joslyn Art Museum, who served as coordinator and copy editor for this volume. Together with the contributing authors, I wish to express deep appreciation to the Nebraska Committee for the Humanities for their sponsorship of the symposium and to the National Endowment for the Humanities, whose generous support made publication of the symposium papers a reality.

Hollister Sturges

The Rural Vision
France and America
in the Late Nineteenth Century

The Urban Vision of the Countryside in Late Nineteenth-Century French Painting

An Essay on Art and Political Culture

by Robert J. Bezucha

THE distinction between urban and rural is central to Western culture. As Raymond Williams notes, "Country and city are very powerful words, and this is not surprising when one remembers how much they seem to stand for in the experience of human communities."[1] They are more than words, however. They are also complex clusters of images whose interpretation is neither historically permanent nor universally accepted. It follows, therefore, that the urban vision of the countryside, whether it is expressed through the formal codes of art or by the ordinary signs of daily life, has not only been different at different times, but also can be different for different persons at the *same* time. Here, as contrasting examples, are two mid-nineteenth-century texts. The first was written by a rural wage-laborer:

> When we were done with Mr. Scott, we were hired at half-a-crown a day to mow the grass within Duddingston policies (domain or home park). The place belonged to the Marquis of Abercorn, but he seldom lives there, at least not then. But there was a fashionable party of ladies and gentlemen, and ladies and lords, staying at the house, and we were not allowed to mow near the mansion in the morning before ten or eleven o'clock, lest the whetting of our scythes might disturb them in bed. When the day was further advanced they used to come out, walk among the hay, and look at us. The ladies were elegant creatures, but I would have thought more of them had they not said frequently in our hearing, "How nice it is to be a mower! how I should like to be always a-haymaking!" The innocent creatures knew no better.[2]

The second was written by Karl Marx:

> The small-holding peasants form a vast mass, the members of which live in similar conditions but without entering into manifold relations with one another. . . . A small-holding,

a peasant and his family; alongside them another small holding, another peasant and another family. A few score of these make up a village, and a few score of villages make up a Department. In this way, the great mass of the French nation is formed by the simple addition of homologous magnitudes, much as potatoes in a sack form a sack of potatoes.[3]

One can trace the polarity of the pastoral and the polis back as far as classical antiquity, but it is essential to recognize that it took on new and powerful meanings in the nineteenth century in the face of the introduction of universal male suffrage in France in 1848 and the transforming social and economic processes which we today describe as urbanization, industrialization, and agrarian capitalism. The various ways that the shifting urban vision of the changing countryside found expression in oil painting leads us to the subject of Realism as an artistic style and to the exhibition on *Jules Breton and the French Rural Tradition* at the Joslyn Art Museum.

The general topic of the museum's opening symposium was the relationship between artistic representation and the realities of rural life. This is a difficult and important problem, an enduring question in the social history of art. I want to begin this essay, therefore, with an illustration of how professional training determines the way we initially "read" a painting—or an entire exhibition. By revealing my own *déformation professionnele* from the start, I hope to make clear to the reader what I consider to be my role in this collection.

Recently I was reading selections from Cora-Elizabeth Millet-Robinet's *La Maison rustique des dames,* a popular manual for women who supervised rural households which went through twenty-one editions between 1844 and 1920. I came upon the following passage: "The distribution of alms should be carried out exclusively by the wife; this is, for her, a most sweet and just reward for all the trouble she takes."[4] I thought immediately of Gustave Courbet's painting *The Village Maidens Giving Alms to a Cowherd,* which portrays the artist's three sisters with their pet dog in the middle of a pasture handing something to a young girl who is tending her cows. The Courbet sisters are dressed in the store-bought gowns and hats and carry the parasols which not only signal their high status in the rural community, but also contrast with the simple homemade garb of the peasant receiving their charity. I do not know for certain that there actually was a copy of *La Maison rustique des dames* in the Courbet household (although they were precisely the sort of family for whom it was intended), but when I linked Millet-Robinet's words with Courbet's painting in my mind, what had previously seemed a strange scene suddenly looked obvious: here were the daughters of the rural bourgeoisie practicing polite behavior in preparation for the day when they would become wives and managers of a household. Courbet's canvas became a specific statement about class relations and gender roles in mid-nineteenth-century France.

I shared my observation the following evening with Robert Herbert, Professor of Art History at Yale University, and his response was to begin to recite a list of European paintings that portray the giving of alms, starting with Rembrandt and ending with Courbet. Although I was at first discouraged and convinced that somehow I had made a foolish mistake, I later realized that each of us might be correct in our own way. When I look at a painting, my training as an historian causes me to think about it as a social product of a specific time and place, to engage it within the broad realm of culture and society. Herbert's training as an art historian, on the other hand, leads him initially to seek an artistic explanation for art, to engage a painting in the narrower realm of craft and the iconographic tradition. What I took to be a disagreement over interpretation was, in fact, the breakdown of a dialogue between two equally valid modes of analysis, neither of which is completely satisfactory. In this case we failed in our conversation because we were unable to transcend our separate first "readings" of Courbet's visual text. I propose that if we are ever going to write a true social history of nineteenth-century art we—the historian and the art historian— must learn to listen to one another and begin to generate a dialogue that respects both perspectives and explores how to hold them simultaneously in creative tension.[5]

In this essay I intend to focus on a rather specific question: how can we explain the widespread popularity of oil paintings with peasant subjects in France in the 1880s? I will be discussing precisely the kind of art represented in *Jules Breton and the French Rural Tradition:* paintings which for at least the past fifty years have been ridiculed by museum staffs and art experts as being old-fashioned and the epitome of what is bad about "bourgeois art." In 1934, Jules Breton's *The Song of the Lark* [fig. 36] won a newspaper popularity poll, and the director the Art Institute of Chicago responded by having the canvas returned to storage. "It's not good enough," he later wrote. "That's why it's not hanging. In a weak moment during the world's fair we showed it because it was voted America's most popular painting. That shows the poor taste of America."[6] How are we to explain the current revival of interest in Breton's work in the face of such hearty scorn? The answer, of course, lies in the vicissitudes of art history practice.

The career of Jules Breton (1827-1906) once seemed a great success story. It began with early triumphs: his work was in the Luxembourg Museum when he was thirty and on the cover of France's first weekly illustrated magazine when he was thirty-two. It lasted for a long time: he participated in the birth of Realism and outlasted most of the Impressionists, all the while continuing to paint scenes of peasant life, most of them set in or around his native village of Courrières in the Artois. Breton exhibited in the Paris Salon forty-six times between 1849 and 1905, including twenty-seven consecutive years after the age of fifty-two. He was a member of the Salon jury for twenty years. Breton's life was filled with official distinction: he won many Salon medals, was awarded the Legion of Honor, and elected to the Institute of France in 1886; his paintings were shown as representative of the best in French art at the Universal Expositions of 1867, 1878, 1889, and 1900. And it was also financially rewarding: in 1886 *The Communicants* sold at auction in New York for $45,000; this was the largest sum ever paid for the work of a living artist, with the exception of Meissonier. Within a few decades after his death, however, art experts were hiding Breton's canvases in the basement. (Gerald Ackerman informs me that Gérôme's *The Age of Augustus* [1855] was rolled up and forgotten, and in its place the staff of the municipal museum of Amiens hung color reproductions of Monet and Renoir, as if to apologize for the deficiency of their collection.[7]) *Sic transit gloria mundi.* Breton shared the fate of Gérôme, Bouguereau, Cabanel, and Meissonier. The reputation of these mighty generals of nineteenth-century Salon painting plummeted with the victory of the avant-garde insurgents. They are the victims of Modernism. And most art historians today think they asked for it.

The art history establishment has made an enormous investment in Modernism—and in the modernist discourse about painting as well. Modern art and its precursors, particularly Courbet and Manet, are now considered the winning side. Dusting off Salon painting has been interpreted by some scholars as a minor act of *lèse-majesté*, treason toward the once embattled and now established status of the avant-garde artist. Sustaining the military-political analogy, they consider shows such as *Jules Breton and the French Rural Tradition* a distasteful expression of counterrevolutionary sentiment. Taste, however, can be an obstacle to writing serious history of any sort. It tells us more about our own time than it does about the past.

The revival of interest in Breton's work began in this country in 1980 with *The Realist Tradition: French Painting and Drawing, 1830-1900,* an exhibition organized by Gabriel P. Weisberg. The critics were almost unanimous in the opinion that the show was all wrong. Kirk Varnedoe's review in *Art in America* was called "Realism's Second String" and featured an editorial lead in bold type that stated "a current large-budget show of French Realism neglects the movement's avant-garde heroes and favors, instead, an idiosyncratic selection of minor masters"—like Breton, who was represented eighteen times.[8] *The Realist Tradition* had gaps and flaws to be sure, but polite ridicule and condescension could not obscure the fact, as even the harshest critics acknowledged, that Weisberg was challenging us to look at a different version of nineteenth-century art than the one with which we have become familiar.

Jules Breton and the French Rural Tradition, organized by Hollister Sturges at the Joslyn Art Museum in Omaha, allows us to sustain and refine the initial effort of reassessment by concentrating on a single, important painter. It matters, therefore, how we respond to the exhibition. It would be a mistake, I believe, to attempt to restore Breton to his former status. He may have been a hero in his own day (to use *Art News* lingo), but I doubt that he ever will become one in ours. Instead, we should come to terms with him historically; we need to use our eyes and minds to try to understand the considerable reputation he enjoyed during his lifetime. It is in that spirit that I offer the following remarks about the popularity of peasant paintings in the 1880s.

Let me begin by establishing the importance of rural images in the cultural life of France at that time, and then place them within the context of current art history practice. My larger purpose is to contribute some ideas toward an understanding of later Realism—Realism in the era we have been taught to think about as the age of the Impressionists. My perspective, as I explained earlier, is that of a social historian.

Our first step must be to leave the art museum itself and to abandon the pursuit of the masterpiece, which so dominates and distorts the experience of the average museum visitor. It has been estimated that around 200,000 oil paintings were produced in France in each decade of the last half of the nineteenth century—one million paintings during the span of Breton's career![9] I want to redirect our attention to some of the obscure artists who poured out countless rural scenes intended for commercial sale to men and women for whom an original canvas in the salon, the dining room, or the bedroom was a clear mark of social status. Virtually none of these paintings have ever hung in a museum, and those that survive remain in the hands of the descendants of their original owners. Some come to light, however, in the auction catalogues of Sotheby's and other dealers, where they are purchased as financial investments and symbols of success by persons who cannot afford to compete in the high-stakes contest to own "great" art. What is striking when we compare the work of a major painter, such as Jules Breton, side-by-side with the work of forgotten men, such as Aimé Perret and Georges Laugée [figs. 1 and 2], is that it all looks so much alike. Breton's superior talent is evident, to be sure, but to an historian's untrained eye these artists share a tone and vision. Their paintings are similar as cultural images. The distinction between "museum art" and "art-that-is-not-in-museums" (to choose from among a number of awkward terms) has always been a serious problem in art history because of the constant tug toward connoisseurship. That, I suspect, is why we lack an adequate word to describe it.

Breton's influence on other artists was probably at its height in the 1880s. Not only were his paintings lauded by the *Salonniers* and bought for huge prices, but also when he retired as a senior member of the Salon jury, he was immediately elected to the prestigious Institute, the first Realist to be so honored. His vision of rural life set the standard for the educated urban public, the bourgeois readers of *L'Illustration*. And he was not the only peasant-painter to be recognized by the same Third Republic government that by and large ignored the Impressionists. In 1889, Breton's obvious disciple, Julien Dupré [fig. 3], stood in the shadow of the new Eiffel Tower at the Universal Exposition to receive a gold medal for his artistic dedication to scenes of rural labor.[10]

Fig. 1. Aimé Perret, *The Gleaner,* oil on canvas, 24 × 19½ in. Photo © 1987 Sotheby's, Inc.

Fig. 2. Georges François Paul Laugée, *The Gleaners,* 1882, oil on canvas, 26 × 32 in. Photo © 1987 Sotheby's, Inc.

Fig. 3. Julien Dupré, *Haying Scene,* 1882, 25⅝ × 31¾ in. Washington University Gallery of Art, St. Louis.

From the vulgar perspective of the marketplace (a place where historians are more likely to be found than art historians), one can suggest that so many artists produced peasant scenes in the 1880s because they were popular and socially acceptable, particularly if they looked like the work of Jules Breton. Peasants sold paintings, in other words, and later I will attempt to explain why.

Let us now turn to current art history practice and examine three statements about change in nineteenth-century French painting. In his article "City vs. Country: The Rural Image in French Painting from Millet to Gauguin," Robert Herbert notes, "In the quarter century following Millet's death in 1875, peasant subjects enjoyed a widespread popularity never before equaled. . . . [It] became commonplace for railroad magnates and industrial leaders to surround themselves with peasants and rural scenery." Herbert sees these paintings as objects intended to inspire relaxation. Looking at them was a means to escape from the cares of modern life. He contrasts this late-nineteenth-century "industrial sensibilit[y]" with that of Millet's day, when Realist peasant-paintings were considered controversial and unsettling because French peasants themselves were "objects of passionate social concern as victims of the massive displacements of the urban-industrial revolution."[11] By this interpretation, the meaning of the rural image (or, more accurately, the *urban* image of the countryside) changed in oil painting between the start of the Second Empire (1851) and the early decades of the Third Republic.

In her important and influential book, *Realism,* Linda Nochlin offers support for Herbert's opinion by pointing out that "realism, as a vital and progressive movement in art, begins to lose steam in the eighties." A generation earlier Realist painters had constituted the avant garde in oil painting, but about the time Breton left the Salon jury and entered the Institute, their work had lost its cutting edge and the style itself was not considered to be in the best taste. In the process, Nochlin suggests, "some of its qualities were transvalued."[12] Not only had Realism sacrificed most of its earlier ability to record social concern, but also it had become a means of expressing bourgeois contentment.

John Berger offers one explanation for the transvaluation of Realist values in his essay "Millet and the Peasant." The "language of oil painting" was inadequate to the task in the long run, he contends. There was "no formula for representing the close, harsh patient physicality of the peasant's labor *on*, instead of *in front of,* the land. . . . And to invent one," he adds, "would mean destroying the traditional language for depicting scenic landscape."[13] Realism failed to sustain itself in confronting the reality of peasant life, Berger maintains, because the canons of oil painting would not permit it. The medium, in other words, eventually undercut and co-opted the initial message of Realism.

What had begun as a *movement* around 1848, a radical challenge to established art practice in an era of political and social revolution, had become an acceptable *style* by the 1880s. The general appearance of peasant paintings changed as a result. The question is why. The art historians I have just cited point to the inherent limitations of the painterly tradition (Berger), the petering out of the avant garde (Nochlin), and the emergence of a new role for art as a private icon that protected its owner from the psychological strains of industrial society (Herbert). The complex terrain of this argument helps us to explain why late Realism surrendered to what Charles Rosen and Henri Zerner have called its "trio of enemies: the sentimental, the picturesque, and the anecdotal."[14] Except for the broad reference to industrialization and urbanization, however, it does little to satisfy my earlier question about the wide-spread popularity of peasant scenes in the 1880s. In the next section of this essay, I will attempt my own answer by engaging artistic subject and style within social history in a discussion of the political culture of the early Third Republic.

There is a cliché among historians that the Third Republic lasted so long (until 1939) because it was the form of government that divided Frenchmen least. Born out of a series of compromises with the divided monarchists and the disgraced Bonapartists following the national humiliation of the Franco-Prussian war, the new regime was timid from the start. The bloody suppression of the Paris Commune by the French army in 1871—Marx called it "the Civil War in France"—made many Republicans, particularly those who held public office, anxious to dispel any notion that they intended to take up where their forefathers had left off in 1793 and 1848. The adoption of the tri-colored flag and the establishment of 14 July as the national holiday were enough reminders of revolution for these men. The Third Republic needed a new symbol of its own, and it found what it was looking for in the peasantry.

In a banquet speech in 1884, the year Breton painted *The Song of the Lark,* Jules Ferry proclaimed, "The Republic will be a peasant's republic or it will cease to exist."[15] Ferry was the political father of the modern French public school system, the person principally responsible for bringing free and obligatory primary education to every village. He and Léon Gambetta, who established France's first Ministry of Agriculture in 1881, were deeply committed to improving the lives of her ordinary rural citizens. (Breton mentions Gambetta's influence on his own life in his autobiography, *La Vie d'un Artiste.*[16]) The following table is drawn from the results of the Agricultural Inquiry of 1882, and it makes clear the size of the problem these reformers faced; in interpreting it one should keep in mind that only farms over fifteen hectares (approximately thirty-seven acres) could be worked by a single family for profit rather than for personal subsistence, and that in 1892, three-quarters of all French farms were still less than ten hectares:[17]

The Distribution of French Farmland in 1882

	Number	Surface (in hectares)	Average Size
Less than one hectare	2,167,667	1,083,833	.499
1-10 hectares	2,635,274	11,366,274	4.313
10-40 hectares	727,088	14,845,274	20.414
More than 40 hectares	142,088	22,266,104	156.706

The human reality behind these numbers is unavoidable. The "peasant's republic" that Ferry dreamed of creating one day was then composed, not of a bulwark of sturdy and independent rural families, but of a welter of dependent sharecroppers, tenant farmers, hired hands, farm servants, and day laborers in an agricultural system dominated by a relatively small number of large farms and great estates. Each year scores of thousands of these poor people were giving up on the land and heading for France's cities and factories.

Moreover, Ferry and Gambetta were exceptions. Most

politicians of the period ignored the actual condition of the "peasantry" while at the same time extolled the natural moral order of an imaginary countryside which official rhetoric proclaimed to be classless and egalitarian. It was during the early decades of the Third Republic that the political myth was born (it remains one of the most persistent errors in the "official" version of French history) that the destruction of the *ancien régime* by the Revolution of 1789 had created a new nation whose people lived free from exploitation and in which a century later their government oversaw the fulfillment of the motto "Liberty, Equality, Fraternity." Gordon Wright has described the political culture of this period as "peasantism," and Theodore Zeldin has resorted to the phrase "the duping of the peasants" to identify the complex ideological process through which the invented virtues of the majority of French voters (rural males) were routinely praised while their real interests were systematically ignored.[18]

Realism was not the only thing to be transvalued in the 1880s. As the Third Republic weathered a string of scandals and political crises—the Boulanger Affair, the Panama Scandal, the Wilson Scandal, and finally the Dreyfus Affair—the evident apathy of the rural poor over the latest news of Parisian politics was no longer considered a subject of serious concern and became instead a source of solace to the moderate Republicans. In 1898, for example, a rural commissioner near Limoges reported to the Prefect of the Creuse Department that "the situation is absolutely different in the countryside. . . . [The Dreyfus Affair] has barely touched those who live their lives isolated and who occupy themselves with calm work in the fields."[19] By the end of the century, in other words, the very characteristics of rural life that Marx had ridiculed and that Courbet and Millet thought were expressions of the peasants' victimization had been transformed into civic qualities which it was implicitly hoped that the urban poor would emulate.

The passage of time, moreover, provides a common-sense dimension to the interaction between artistic style and political culture. The critical reaction to the *early* Realist portrayal of peasant life was deeply influenced by the recent memory of rural violence. Jean Rousseau thought he caught sight of "the pikes of popular uprisings . . . outlined on the leaden horizon" of Millet's *Gleaners* (1857) [fig. 39], for example, because the grain riots of 1846 and 1847, and the massive rural resistance to Louis Napoleon's coup d'état, had frightened the wits out of the bourgeoisie. I am certain that Breton's initial popularity—from the Emperor, who bought his *Recall*

of the Gleaners (1859) [fig. 33], to the readers of *L'Illustration,* who saw it on the cover of the magazine in a wood engraving—was due in large measure to his harmonious vision of rural society. The Realist avant garde looked at the countryside and saw the poor; Breton (in his own words) saw "the humble," much to the relief of many people. About the only thing one ever saw outlined on the horizon in Breton's work was the church steeple of Courrières.[20] And by the 1880s, not only were Courbet and Millet both dead, but also it was more difficult for contemporaries to associate the countryside with insurrection—since there had been none for over a generation. Certainly the portrayal of peasant subjects could still be controversial, as we can witness in the furor over the brutal scenes in Zola's *La Terre* (1887). But Zola is the veritable exception that proves the rule: he had coined the phrase "Naturalism" in 1880 to distinguish what he was attempting from what Realism had become, and he was also among the first critics to recognize the Impressionists as the legitimate artistic descendants of Courbet.[21] By the 1880s, in short, Breton's vision of rural life was the dominant one, and the new regime embraced it.

Listen to the way that Arsène Houssaye praised Breton's *Shepherd's Star* [fig. 4] in his review of the Salon of 1888, only a few months after the publication of Zola's *La Terre*: "With an admirable alliance of the real and the ideal," Houssaye wrote, "this daughter of the fields has become a true peasant; but imagine that she carries on her back a sheaf of wheat instead of a sack of potatoes, and then she could be the personification of harvesting. She would be a modern Ceres."[22] The "true peasant" was now "a modern Ceres," goddess of the harvest, an eternal figure. Gone is the sense of contemporaneity (*"Il faut être de son temps,"* as Daumier had put it) associated with early Realism. Gone, too, is any intimation of the peasant as a "victim," as a member of a rural class which was exploited and suffered at its work. One might respond, of course, by saying that French Salon critics were trained on Greek and Latin literature in the *lycées* and knew their Bible, and therefore were always reading cultural symbols into paintings of rural life. Marx knew what a sack of potatoes looked like, however, and that is why I suspect that Houssaye's remark is more than an ordinary classical allusion. It is better described as a bourgeois *il*lusion which, like Breton's painting itself, was part of the political culture of the early Third Republic.

Let me offer further evidence by mentioning another aspect of late Realist peasant painting: by the 1880s they

Fig. 4. Jules Breton, *The Shepherd's Star,* 1887, oil on canvas, 40½ × 31 in. The Toledo Museum of Art, Gift of Arthur J. Secor.

generally were pictures of women, interchangeable images of feminized rural labor. No more plowmen, sowers, and stone breakers to be found; just milkmaids and their sisters drew the artist's eye. The reasons for this change are obviously complex, and I have mentioned some of them earlier in this essay. To these we might add Linda Nochlin's contention that such paintings served as vehicles for "ideological definitions of femininity" and "the good worker."[23] I also think they functioned as important political symbols as well. Marianne, the fiery female symbol of the Republic before the establishment of France's third attempt at one, was a radical city girl born and reborn on the barricades in 1789, 1830, and 1848. Her maiden name was Liberty, and Delacroix painted her leading the people into revolution. The feminized peasant paintings of the 1880s were alternative images of her country cousins, symbols of calm productive labor and imagined rural stability. As the distinguished French historian Maurice Agulhon has demonstrated in *Marianne into Battle: Republican Imagery and Symbolism in France, 1789-1880,* the political founders of the Third Republic consciously chose a female figure called "the Ceres-Liberty" as the official symbol of the regime for the nation's coins and postage stamps.[24] She, like late Realist peasant women, successfully encased modernity—in this case political modernity—within a cloak of "traditional" values. Neither Marianne, a reminder of urban unrest, nor Joan of Arc, the emerging cult figure of conservatives and monarchists, Ceres-Liberty looked like the women Jules Breton had been painting for thirty years. For better or for worse, history had caught up with him.

By now some readers will have surely concluded the I am guilty of beating art with a political stick, although such crude reductionism was far from my intention. In order to set the record straight, I want to conclude by commenting on a quotation attributed to D. H. Lawrence. "Let me hear what the *novel* says," he wrote. "As for the novelist he is usually a dribbling liar." The connoisseur might equally wish me to stick to the painting (art-as-a-subject-in-and-for-itself) and leave the social history out of it. My response is that Lawrence is right about the individual novelist (or painter), but when the same person is looked at in a wider context, the "lies" he tells in common with his fellow artists are called a *style*—in this case, late Realism—and the ways that style interacts with other elements in a culture—such as the political culture of the early Third Republic—can be used as a step in the direction of understanding the social history of nineteenth-century art.

Notes

1. Raymond Williams, *The Country and the City* (London: Chatto, 1973), pp. 1-2.

2. Alexander Somerville, *Autobiography of a Working Man* (London, 1848), p. 63.

3. Karl Marx, *The 18th Brumaire of Louis Bonaparte* (New York: International Publishers, 1963), pp. 123-24.

4. Cited in *Victorian Women*, eds. Erna Olafson Hellerstein, Leslie Parker Hume, and Karen M. Offen (Stanford: Stanford University Press, 1981), p. 294.

5. For another discussion of explanation in history and art history, see Peter Gay, *Art and Act: On Causes in History—Manet, Gropius, Mondrian* (New York: Harper and Row, 1975), pp. 1-34.

6. Robert Harshe in *Art Institute of Chicago Newsletter*, 19 January 1936, cited by Hollister Sturges in *Jules Breton and the French Rural Tradition* (Omaha, Neb.: Joslyn Art Museum, 1982), p. 95.

7. Personal communication from Professor Ackerman, 15 April 1983.

8. Kirk Varnedoe, "Realism's Second String," *Art in America* (September 1981):134-41.

9. Harrison C. White and Cynthia A. White, *Canvases and Careers: Institutional Change in the French Painting World* (New York: John Wiley & Sons, 1965), p. 83.

10. Gabriel P. Weisberg, *The Realist Tradition: French Painting and Drawing, 1830-1900* (Cleveland: The Cleveland Museum of Art, 1980), p. 287.

11. Robert L. Herbert, "City vs. Country: The Rural Image in French Painting from Millet to Gauguin," *Artforum* 8 (February 1970):44-55.

12. Linda Nochlin, *Realism* (London and New York: Penguin Books, 1971), p. 225.

13. John Berger, "Millet and the Peasant," in *About Looking* (New York: Pantheon Books, 1980), pp. 69-78.

14. Charles Rosen and Henri Zerner, "Enemies of Realism," *The New York Review of Books*, 4 March 1982, p. 31.

15. Cited in Gordon Wright, *Rural Revolution in France: The Peasantry in the Twentieth Century* (Stanford: Stanford University Press, 1964), p. 13.

16. Jules Breton, *La Vie d'un Artiste* (Paris, 1890), p. 177.

17. This table is drawn from Marcel Faure, *Les Paysans dans la société français* (Paris: A. Colin, 1966), p. 17. The material on 1892 comes from Theodore Zeldin, *France, 1848-1945*, 2 vols. (Oxford and New York: Oxford University Press, 1973 and 1977), 1:135.

18. Wright, *Rural Revolution in France*, p. 1, and Zeldin, *France, 1848-1945*, 1:129.

19. I wish to thank Professor Michael Burns of Mt. Holyoke College, who dug this quotation out of the Archives Nationales and gave me permission to cite it.

20. For a discussion of Breton's social consciousness, see my article "Being Realistic about Realism: Art and the Social History of Nineteenth Century France," in ed. Gabriel P. Weisberg, *The European Realist Tradition* (Bloomington: Indiana University Press, 1982), pp. 1-13.

21. For example, see Zola's "Naturalism in the Salon" (1880), in ed. Roland N. Stromberg, *Realism, Naturalism, and Symbolism* (New York: Harper and Row, 1968), pp. 154-62.

22. Cited in Weisberg, ed., *The Realist Tradition*, p. 234.

23. Linda Nochlin, The 'Cribleuses du blé': Courbet, Millet, Breton, Kollwitz and the Image of the Working Woman," in eds. K. Gallwitz and K. Herding, *Malerei und Theorie: Das Courbet Colloquium, 1979* (Frankfurt am Main: Städtlische Galerie im Städelschen Kunstinstitut, 1979), pp. 49-71.

24. Maurice Agulhon, *Marianne Into Battle: Republican Imagery and Symbolism in France, 1789-1880*, trans. Janet Lloyd (Cambridge and New York: Cambridge University Press, 1981), pp. 157, 164.

Fig. 5. François Boucher, *Are They Thinking About the Grape?,* 1747, oil on canvas, 31¾ × 27 in. The Art Institute of Chicago, purchased from Martha E. Leverone Bequest.

Fig. 6. Holman Hunt, *The Hireling Shepherd,* 1851, oil on canvas, 30⅛ × 43⅛ in. City of Manchester Art Galleries, Manchester, England.

Jules Breton
Creator of a Noble Peasant Image

by Hollister Sturges

No peasants have been so closely studied as the French. Since Eugene Bonnemère's first history of the French peasantry, a passionate mid-nineteenth-century account emphasizing the injustices sustained throughout the centuries by the nation's agricultural workforce, economic and social historians have progressively marshaled more facts and statistics in a study of the peasants' productivity, welfare, attitudes, and character.[1] Invariably, such studies make clear the heterogeneity of the peasants as a class.[2] They stress the variance in customs from region to region and the differences in the economic condition of the peasant, who ranged from landless rural laborer or impoverished sharecropper to wealthy landowner and tenant farmer. While the modern historian attempts to draw an accurate objective portrait of the French peasant, from the early Renaissance through the nineteenth century, cultured society perceived the peasant, to judge from characterizations in journals, diaries, and works of art and literature, with little understanding or sympathy. Until the nineteenth century in the realm of fine art and literature, the peasant as a subject was largely ignored, considered too crude and lowly to warrant representation. Important exceptions to this general neglect offer stereotyped images. Dutch painters of the seventeenth century burlesqued the peasant, invariably portraying him as boorish and vulgar, a drunken buffoon carousing in a tavern. To gratify the refined taste of court and urban patrons, artists of eighteenth-century France fabricated countless images of coiffed and beribboned rural personages, a repertoire of comic-opera peasants. Most typical of this seductive vision of bucolic life are the pastorals of François Boucher in such paintings as *Are They Thinking About the Grape?* [fig. 5], which depicts shepherds courting in a scene marked by extreme elegance and artificiality.

A century later the Pre-Raphaelite painter Holman Hunt continued the artistic tradition of depicting country life with an unnatural elegance. Ironically, in his moralizing genre subject, *The Hireling Shepherd* (1851) [fig. 6], Hunt makes a pointed critical reference to the frivolity of Boucher's bucolic scene and the facile manner in which it is rendered. His pastoral picture becomes a sermon on the theme of temptation and neglect, and Hunt's rebuke to the hireling who neglects his flock is intended to extend to Boucher in particular and other such painters who are negligent in their depiction of nature. For Hunt, the antidote to Boucher's artifice is to render natural phenomena, particularly the variety of plant life, with almost maniacal accuracy and detail. Notwithstanding his insistence upon a certain literal truth, Hunt's own picture, with its jewellike colors, glossy painted surfaces, and complex literary symbolism, has an artificiality which belies the naturalistic intentions he professed.[3] His sparkling scene does not attempt a convincing portrayal of authentic peasants, nor does it address itself to the realities of rural life.

Today, we accept as part of our cultural heritage conceptions about peasants and their customs quite different from those suggested by Boucher or Hunt. One cherished conception honors the peasant for the nobility of a life devoted to working the land. This notion can be traced back to an agrarian creed in classical antiquity that was best expressed in Virgil's *Georgics.* During the

Fig. 7. Jules Breton, *The Vintage at Château Lagrange,* 1864, oil on canvas, 35¾ × 66⅛ in. Joslyn Art Museum.

Enlightenment, Jean-Jacques Rousseau gave the notion fresh impetus with his back-to-nature ideas and admiration for the noble savage. Nevertheless, it was not until the mid nineteenth century, when industrialization, urbanization, and large-scale agricultural operations threatened to disrupt the time-honored practices and institutions of rural life, that the peasants and their customs came to be recognized as worthy of wide-spread celebration.[4] In the face of change, western Europe, particularly England, France, and the Netherlands, evolved a set of ideals that emphasized the virtues of country life. A new significance was given to the charm and wholesomeness of rustic ways, to the dignity of living close to the soil, to the beauty of preindustrial landscape, and to the social harmony of the agrarian community. This discussion aims at examining the vision of the artist who gave the fullest expression to these ideals, the French painter Jules Breton.

The noble character of Breton's interpretation of the French peasantry is immediately evident upon viewing his large Paris Salon picture, *The Vintage at Château Lagrange* [fig. 7]. Executed during the Second Napoleonic Empire, this example of Breton's mature style portrays proud, statuesque women from the vineyards near Bordeaux. Significantly, the moment depicted is the end of the day, when the workers are leaving the fields with their crop, a celebration of the bounty of the harvest rather than the toil of field labor. In his memoirs Breton gives us a precise account of the circumstances of the picture's commission and of his own artistic aspirations at this juncture in his career.[5]

In the fall of 1862, at the invitation of the wealthy landowner Count Duchâtel, Breton journeyed to the Médoc region in southwestern France to depict the grape harvest on the count's estate. (The picture was to be a companion piece to Breton's *The Weeders* [fig. 17], already in the count's sizable collection.) Receptive to exploring peasant motifs beyond the area of his native Artois, Breton was eager to travel south, where he dreamed of finding "sublime landscapes with inhabitants embodying types of extraordinary beauty."[6] At Château Lagrange, as was his customary practice, he spent his days observing the activity of the fields, recording it in preparatory drawings and watercolor and oil sketches. Rainy weather and the unfamiliar conditions of the southern light slowed his progress, forcing his return to the Médoc the following fall. Again hampered by grey, wet weather, Breton resorted to observing the vintage by telescope from the château tower and hired a local photographer to document the tasks of the vineyard.[7] Characteristically, his on-the-spot studies depict the activity of the harvesters with an energy and verve not found in the final canvas. Figures possess a muscular tension and turn or twist more actively. In one watercolor [fig. 8], the movement is implicit in the posture of the two central standing women, while there is vigor in the small boy's action, as with sharply bent leg he braces himself to receive a loaded basket.

For the final Salon composition, Breton simplified the forms to achieve a harmony consonant with the classicism of his academic training. Of this phase in his artistic development, he later noted, "I was no longer dreaming of anything but the grand style. I was wondering if the rustic genre could lead me to it."[8] As we can see from his extreme efforts to render accurate and precise studies, the finished picture is not an exercise in academic figure painting, but a synthesis of close observation and idealization modeled after the classicism of Raphael, Poussin, and other recognized masters. In the large canvas Breton proves less interested in depicting the reality of labor than in achieving an ideal of beauty that appropriately glorified the French peasant. To be sure, the painting was commissioned to celebrate the count's estate and, indirectly, its valuable commercial product, but in the context of Breton's work of the 1860s, it must be seen as another paean to the working peasant.

Precedents for Breton's vision of a thriving peasantry are rare. During the first half of the nineteenth century, the only artist to choose the theme for a major composition was the Swiss painter Léopold Robert, whom Bre-

ton acknowledged as "the first to make a serious study of the peasant."[9] Robert's *The Arrival of the Harvesters in the Pontine Marshes* [fig. 26], exhibited with great success at the Paris Salon of 1831 and purchased by the State for its Luxembourg Museum, was admired by Breton from his first visit to Paris in 1846 until the end of his days. Although Robert primarily capitalized on the exotic and picturesque qualities of his merry band of Italian harvesters returning from the fields, Breton praised him for portraying the nobility of humble types and for the rendering of local customs. Robert's classicizing approach to rustic genre was an influential precedent for Breton; both the idealization of Mediterranean peasant women and the oxcart motif were echoed in *The Vintage at Château Lagrange*. While the Swiss artist, trained as a history painter under Jacques-Louis David, deserves credit for breaking with tradition by monumentalizing rustic figures rather than classical heroes, it should be emphasized that his peasants were gay, colorful characters from a foreign land treated in a theatrical manner. A straightforward depiction of ordinary French peasants was not a suitable subject for Robert's generation. As one of his conservative Salon critics observed, "Place this scene in the plains of Beauce and Champaigne, it will become trivial and grotesque, and the more faithfully it is represented, the more trivial and grotesque it will be."[10]

And certainly Breton, a generation later, however

Fig. 8. Jules Breton, Study for *The Vintage at Château Lagrange,* watercolor on paper, 5⅘ × 10 in. Private collection, France.

Fig. 9. Picnic lunch in the wheatfields of Beauce, c. 1905, photograph. Musée des Beaux-Arts, Chartres.

Fig. 10. Jules Breton, *The Departure for the Fields,* 1857, oil on canvas, 25 × 37 in. Private collection, Omaha.

closely he observed his peasants, sufficiently idealized them to avoid too harsh or coarse an interpretation of reality. His pictures portray an altogether different view of the rural laborer than that suggested by a 1905 photograph [fig. 9] of women farmhands from the Beauce region partaking in a picnic lunch.

The vision of Breton's art is grounded in his childhood. Born in 1827 in Courrières, a small village in the agriculturally rich Artois region of northern France, he was the son of a landowner who managed a large estate for the Duke of Duras and who served for a time as an assistant judge for the canton and mayor of the village. According to his memoirs, Breton, although not raised as a peasant, spent a carefree childhood playing in the barnyard and fields with companions of inferior social position. His father sent him to school, where he received a classical education, and at sixteen he went to study painting at the Royal Academy in Ghent and, later, to the Ecole des Beaux-Arts in Paris in the studio of Michel-Martin Dolling. From his formal artistic training, Breton developed his skill as a precise draftsman in the tradition of Davidian neoclassicism and also came to appreciate the merits of narrative painting in the grand style.

His Paris studies were interrupted by the outbreak of the Revolution of 1848. Witness to the bloodshed of the February insurrection, Breton and his fellow art students were swept up by the political and social upheaval that focused unprecedented attention on the dignity and plight of the popular classes. As Breton eloquently put it:

> The causes and consequences of that revolution . . . had a strong influence on our spirits. . . . There was a great upsurge of new efforts. We studied what Gambetta was later to call the new social stratum and the natural setting which surrounded it. We studied the streets and the fields more deeply; we associated ourselves with the passions and feelings of the humble, and art was to do them the honor formerly reserved exclusively for the gods and for the mighty.[11]

His social consciousness aroused by the turmoil of the Revolution, Breton responded with two paintings that depicted the suffering of the urban poor in graphic terms. *Want and Despair* (his Salon debut in 1849), a contemporary melodrama showing the horrors of oppression, was followed a year later by *Hunger*, one of

Fig. 11. Jules Breton, *The Gleaners,* 1854, oil on canvas, 36½ × 54 in. National Gallery of Ireland, Dublin.

the many politically charged pictures of carnage and disaster of that period. However, the young artist's expressions of social protest were short-lived, and by the summer of 1853 he was back in Courrières, where he discovered his true calling.

Breton's renewed contact with rustic life led him to recognize that his deepest sentiments lay with his native land and its inhabitants. In a few lyrical pages of his memoirs, he describes the majesty of the wheat fields, the mysteries of the marsh, the flaming poppy fields, the radiance of dawn, and the somber twilight through which passed the shadowy figures of peasant girls. The days of reverie and strolling in the fields to observe bands of gleaners evoked memories of a childhood spent in a rustic paradise, the recollection of which was to be the wellspring of his art throughout his life.[12]

Breton's first efforts in this new direction were light-hearted, charming scenes of pretty young women and children in agreeable outdoor settings. Pictures such as *Love Tokens* (c. 1854) and *Departure for the Fields* (1857) [fig. 10] should be considered an updated nineteenth-century version of the pastoral mode, a celebration of leisure activities in idyllic natural surroundings. His most important painting of this type, *The Gleaners* [fig. 11], exhibited at the 1855 Salon, again portrays country life in Arcadian terms. Here, gleaning is presented as a social gathering under open skies, as women and children, working cheerfully in concert, gather the last grains from the freshly harvested plain of Courrières. Their lively and varied poses and the sparkling sunshine of a summer afternoon make light of the burden of their labors. The artist suppresses any suggestion of the drudgery of such toil and allows no hint of misery to spoil his idyll. The open, spacious compositions, blond tonality, and vivid accents of color make this early group of Breton's paintings particularly inviting. Breton's critics admired these delightful country vignettes for their "grace and naïveté" and "innocence and simplicity," responding to them in much the same way critics of the mid eighteenth century responded to the pastorals of Boucher. To be sure, Breton's works avoid the extreme artificiality of Boucher by rendering peasants in a highly individualized manner with genuine costumes and by placing them in specific, often recognizable locales. Still, the impetus behind these pictures comes from his romantic yearning to depict beauty rather than from any desire to render a transcript of country life in realistic terms. In his memoirs, Breton nostalgically echoes this impulse when he asks rhetorically, "What has become of those women gleaners who used to walk barefoot and upright in their splendid rags, their loose hair ripened like the corn in the sun, mingling with the golden gleanings against a blue sky."[13]

During his extended stay in Courrières in the mid 1850s, Breton began his lifelong practice of making outdoor oil studies of landscape motifs. In small, unpretentious sketches, as in *Plain at Courrières, Rainbow at Courrières* (1855), and *Village Houses: Meadows,* his propensity for the flat, cultivated landscape is revealed. While many contemporaries sought more spectacular scenery, such as Alpine vistas or picturesque woodlands, Breton was happy to render the plains of his homeland, the fields of Artois rich in wheat and rye and such commercially profitable crops as flax, poppies, and colza.

Fig. 12. Jules Breton, *The Blessing of the Wheat in Artois,* 1857, oil on canvas, 50½ × 125¼ in. Museé d'Orsay, Paris.

Fig. 13. Gustave Courbet, *The Burial at Ornans,* 1849, oil on canvas, 123 ¾ × 261 in. Museé d'Orsay, Paris.

With particular sensitivity to effects of light, he depicts vast stretches of his native terrain, its abundant crops, working peasants, and great skies.

Along with *plein-air* sketches and pastoral scenes set in the environs of Courrières, Breton executed two large compositions in an effort to transform rural subject matter into a monumental art. His most ambitious canvas up to this time, *The Blessing of the Wheat in Artois* [fig. 12], exhibited at the 1857 Salon, translates the customs of this rural community on an epic scale that clearly aims at rivaling Gustave Courbet's great picture, *The Burial at Ornans* [fig. 13], the Salon sensation seven years earlier that provoked both outrage and acclaim. Like Courbet, Breton gathered all segments of village society in a religious ceremony. While both artists organized their figures in a friezelike arrangement and incorporated portraits and a wealth of closely observed detail to give their work a sense of authenticity, their interpretations of events are opposed. Courbet's unsentimental, even harsh depiction of a country funeral interprets death in secular terms. There is little to suggest the inspiration of the divine or the transcendence of the spirit. By contrast, in his rendering of a priestly procession on the plain of Courrières, Breton emphasized that the Christian faith of the community was still intact. In this ancient, rustic ritual intended to assure the abundance of the harvest, the priest beneath the canopy carries the host in the monstrance out into the fields. Rural notables, village maidens, and others make up the procession, and

as they pass, peasants kneel before them in pious gratitude. This epic picture emphasizes the social harmony of the agricultural community, which in turn brings forth the fruits of a bountiful nature.

Breton's conception of the peasant seems conditioned primarily by the prominent social position within the community he occupied since birth. The Breton family were bourgeois, at the top of the social hierarchy of their canton. They belonged to a class which Alain Morel, in his well-documented study "Power and Ideology in the Village Community of Picardy: Past and Present," called the "rural notables."[14] As leading members of the bourgeoisie, they had the privileges of wealth and power. Their education gave them access to both French culture and the advanced scientific discoveries of agriculture. Within their village they were the source of information, the arbiters of justice, the patrons of jobs and promotions, and the dispensers of charity. Rural notables did not work with their hands. They were the employer class and used their influence to promote an ideology that preserved their interests and enhanced the respect and obedience they commanded. Key points of this ideology, as articulated by Morel, include the obligation of each class to fulfill its duties, thereby contributing to an overall harmony, and the paternalistic role of the employer who teaches the workers "how to honor a contract and how to accept their station in life."[15] This ideology also stresses "the Christian order of things, based as it is on religion, family and property, [which]

Fig. 14. Jules Breton, *Wine Shop—Monday,* 1858, oil on canvas, 39¾ × 43⅜ in. Washington University Gallery of Art, St. Louis.

will provide workers with moral satisfaction.''[16] As the old order became progressively threatened by industrial development, its values had to be vigorously defended and preserved.[17]

Breton's own words condemning social progress correspond almost exactly to Morel's account of nineteenth-century paternalism in rural France. In *Un Peintre paysan,* published in 1896, Breton wrote:

> I do not see that people are happier today. On the contrary, in the old days they were poorer, but they had fewer needs, and they more fully enjoyed the natural treasures which providence never absolutely devours and which, in the end, are the most precious. They submitted to the imperial law of individual and social inequality, and each found in this resignation a great contentment with his fate.[18]

The peasants he depicts in *The Blessing of the Wheat* are perceived from the vantage point of his superior social position. Again, his own description of them speaks for itself.

> Here are those peasants who smiled at me during my childhood. They walk, heads slightly lowered, their steps slow,

murmuring psalms, their minds lost in vague mysteries that disturb them not at all; they go, peacefully, in their best clothes, over that road that has soaked up their sweat . . . they go imploring for their humble households only happiness without trouble, daily bread from their work, health, and honor; they go thanking Providence whose image they are piously following, in the monstrance shining in the rays of the sun.[19]

Humble, pious, hard-working, and above all content with their lot, Breton's peasants exemplify harmonious social relations between master and worker. His other important canvas of this period, *Fire in a Haystack,* also carries a social message. In this treatment of a blazing fire under the midday sun, Breton chose to emphasize the cooperative efforts of the peasants to extinguish the flames and salvage the crop. In lieu of despair, the painting becomes a testament, as Madeleine Fidell-Beaufort has pointed out, to ''the positive values of rural solidarity.''[20]

Motivated by his desire to celebrate and uphold the values of a traditional agrarian community, at this juncture in his career Breton succeeded in portraying peasants with dignity and respect. Only in the next decade, however, in the 1860s, did he achieve an image of the peasant that can be considered heroic.

A key year in Breton's development was 1859. Of the four paintings he exhibited that year at the Salon, *The Recall of the Gleaners* [fig. 33] was best received by the public and critics.[21] Here, proud and dignified peasant women, bathed in the golden half-light of the setting sun, return from the fields at the call of the *garde-champêtre*. The trio of principal figures (suggesting the three ages of womankind), larger proportionally than those found in his early works, and the evening hour create a solemn mood not previously realized by Breton. Almost unanimous in their approval of this work, Salon reviewers commended Breton for achieving a perfect balance between observed reality and poetic sentiment. Characteristic of orthodox critical opinion are the remarks of Henri Delaborde, painter, Salon reviewer, and author two years earlier of a much-discussed book on public taste. He began by distinguishing Breton from Courbet and the Realist school, explaining the difference

in their work as that "which exists between effigies of brute fact and poetic truth, between the literal transcription of a patois and the style of an eclogue." Above all, he commended Breton as the first painter to successfully "represent the rustic types of our country without slandering or idealizing them beyond measure. . .without false nobility or ugliness."[22]

Other commentators corroborated these points. The novelist Alexandre Dumas admired Breton's robust peasant women, who were free from the ugliness of Courbet's female figures and from the prettiness of Boucher's comic-opera shepherdesses.[23] Paul Sainte-Victoire, who two years earlier condemned Millet's *Gleaners* as the "Three Fates of pauperism," perceived Breton as being "rustic without ugliness. . .popular without triviality,"[24] while the distinguished critic Paul Mantz praised him for approaching "the relative ideal which is appropriate to his rustic epics."[25]

However, Paris reviewers expressed reservations about another 1859 Salon entry, *Wine Shop—Monday* [fig. 14],

Fig. 15. Jules Breton, *The Rapeseed Harvest,* 1860, oil on canvas, 37 × 54 in. The Corcoran Gallery of Art, William A. Clark Collection, Washington, D.C.

Fig. 16. Gustave Courbet, *The Grain Sifters,* 1854, oil on canvas, 51½ × 65 ¾ in. Museé de Beaux-Arts, Nantes. (Photo: B. Voisin)

which was decidedly Realistic in orientation. An anec-dotal tavern scene in the Dutch genre tradition, the pic-ture shows a different side of Breton as an observer of comic manners. The humor and vulgarity of the subject allowed little opportunity for idealization, and critics urged the artist to abandon such endeavors.[26] From cor-respondence to his wife, Elodie, we know that Breton paid attention to these opinions. He saved clippings of Salon reviews on his work and even visited critics to dis-cuss their views on art.[27] At this juncture, when Breton faced the choice of emphasizing the realistic or idealis-tic qualities of his art, it seems fair to conclude that the overwhelming encouragement he received to pursue an ennobled vision of French rural life contributed to shap-ing the direction of his work. In the next few years, he developed his peasant images in a style that became pro-gressively more classicized.

In the 1860s Breton sought to reconcile his peasant subjects with the grand tradition of the past by looking to classical and Renaissance sources. Continuing in the direction that he had taken in *The Recall of the Gleaners,* he emphasized the commanding presence of the human figure within a gently evocative landscape. The pic-turesque aspects of rural life—children's play, religious processions, and tavern escapades—gave way to the more sober themes of work in the fields. And the peas-ant women of Artois, so gay and charming in his early pastoral mode, now achieve, through their labor and their close contact with nature, a moral grandeur and serenity. To create an effective image of a proud and noble peasantry, Breton's style became gradually more austere. The bright tonalities and lively color of his early works were muted; the compositions, rarely of great complexity, were further simplified; and the wealth of eye-catching detail, which enlivened his first rustic scenes, was largely eliminated. Precise drawing con-tinued to assure solidity of form, but without the same attention to surface and texture.

The Rapeseed Harvest [fig. 15], exhibited at the 1861 Salon, exemplifies the new aim of Breton's work. The carriage and gesture of the central figure sifting seed possess all the majesty of the grand style. A comparison of this woman with another carrying out a similar action in Courbet's *The Grain Sifters* [fig. 16] makes Breton's idealization of hard labor all the more apparent. Courbet's sifter is depicted from the back, kneeling, her head bent and her legs and arms splayed at awkward angles. Breton's worker stands, head held high, bearing her load with ease. He is more interested in depicting an ideal of beauty appropriate to a noble race of French peasants than in documenting the hardships of work in the fields. To this purpose, he cast his rustic heroines into established classical molds. Emulating the simplicity of form and restrained movement of the Venuses and the Cereses of antiquity and the Renaissance, Breton conferred upon his peasants a dignity and grandeur that made them acceptable in high art. With the exception of Breton's subject matter, the objectives of his art essentially conform to the academic teachings of the day, and as a result, his work is less bold and original than Courbet's. But to his contemporaries, Breton's paintings signified a new vision of the common man. As more than one critic noted, no longer were the peasants to be considered a race apart.[28]

Without question, the painter of rural life who bears the closest comparison to Breton, and hence best clarifies his vision, is Jean-François Millet (1814-1875). As the son of peasant farmers in Normandy, and as one who had actually worked the land, Millet approached the peasant in terms of his labor. Fundamentally, his art is an act of empathy with the travails of the peasant, and his own words convey the seriousness of his intentions.

> Sometimes, in places where the land is sterile, you see figures hoeing and digging. From time to time one raises himself and straightens his back, as they call it, wiping his forehead with the back of his hand. "Thou shalt eat thy bread in the sweat of thy brow." Is this the gay, jovial work some people would have us believe in? But, nevertheless, to me it is true humanity and great poetry.[29]

In his masterpiece, *The Gleaners* (Salon 1857) [fig. 39], Millet emphasizes the pain and fatigue of the peasant's life struggle. The stooped postures, repetitive gestures, and unidealized features of his figures portray the monotony and arduousness of their toil. For him, the "common and melancholy lot of humanity [is] weariness."[30]

By contrast, Breton's most acclaimed painting of women laboring in the fields, *The Weeders* (Salon 1861) [fig. 17], creates a mood of serene beauty during the twilight hour. Across the plain, silhouetted against the sun vanishing on the horizon, several women on their knees, as if in prayer (according to Breton), pull weeds from the soil. The simplicity of these stooped figures hugging the

Fig. 17. Jules Breton, *The Weeders,* 1860, oil on canvas, 37½ × 67 in. Joslyn Art Museum.

Fig. 18. Jules Breton, *The Close of the Day,* 1865, oil on canvas, 25 ¾ × 19 in. Walters Art Gallery, Baltimore.

Fig. 19. Jean-François Millet, *Woman with a Rake,* oil on canvas, 15⅝ × 13½ in. The Metropolitan Museum of Art, Gift of Stephen C. Clark, 1938.

earth conveys a vision of eternal harmony. A single standing figure, observing the setting sun, makes explicit the contemplative mood of twilight. Breton's peasants are both part of and conscious of the mysterious beauty of evening. While for Millet the peasants' concentration on their tasks is primary, for Breton it is their absorption in the mood of poetic reverie.

No painting better embodies Breton's aspirations to a grand vision of the peasant than *Close of the Day,* exhibited at the 1865 Salon, of which there is a replica of the two central figures in the Walters Art Gallery [fig. 18]. Against an evening sky, two statuesque haymakers stand amidst a field of hayricks. Both are calm and pensive: the dominant figure is shown in striking profile with arms crossed, the other leaning upon a rake. A low vantage point makes us look up at them against the horizon, where their silhouettes blend to form an imposing pyramid. The pride and majesty of these figures is underscored when they are compared with Millet's solitary peasant in *Woman with a Rake* [fig. 19]. Whereas Millet's figure, with head bowed and shaded, is seen as humble and self-effacing, Breton, for all his idealization, individualizes the features of his women. In terms of critical success, the painting represents the apogee of

Breton's career. Gautier spoke for most everyone when he praised the painter "for knowing how to disengage the ideal" from subjects taken from reality. He credited Breton for portraying an image of the peasant contrary to La Bruyère's dehumanized creature and for rendering pure types, from which he has extracted "a fresh, healthy, robust beauty, but not without refinement."[31] The conservative Paul Mantz praised the sureness and grandeur of Breton's drawing and stressed that "this simple genre picture had as much character and style" as any history painting at the Salon.[32] The liberal Théophile Thoré, an ardent democrat who had been in political exile during the Second Empire, admired how beauty of form and expression could be united in the rude inhabitants of the countryside. "It is through reality well interpreted," he wrote, "that modern art will rediscover all the allegories—originally inspired by nature. This gentle Breton . . .who pleases everybody. . .shows us in what sense art could develop today."[33] For his contemporaries, Breton's classicized peasants had such universal appeal that they could function as icons of traditional order or as effective symbols of republican ideals.

A comparison of drawings from the mid sixties by Breton and Millet points out another important difference

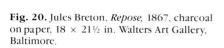

Fig. 20. Jules Breton, *Repose,* 1867, charcoal on paper, 18 × 21½ in. Walters Art Gallery, Baltimore.

Fig. 21. Jean-François Millet, *Noonday Rest (Meridian),* 1867-69, pastel, 28¾ × 38¼ in. Philadelphia Museum of Art, the William L. Elkins Collection.

Fig. 22. Jean-François Millet, *The Potato Harvest,* 1855, oil on canvas, 21¼ × 25⅝ in. Walters Art Gallery, Baltimore.

between these artists: their sense of decorum. In *Repose* [fig. 20], Breton's peasant woman sits absorbed in her thoughts in a graceful pose reminiscent of that of a Greek philosopher. By contrast, in *Noonday Rest* [fig. 21] Millet's figure, sprawled on his back, legs apart and crotch thrust forward, flaunts a vulgarity impermissible in the grand style. As Gautier noted early in the artist's career, "M. Millet's painting has everything that is required to irk the smooth shaven bourgeois. . . . It would be impossible to find anything more rugged and bristly, more savage and uncouth."[34]

Among the nine pictures Millet exhibited at the 1867 Universal Exhibition in Paris was *The Potato Harvest* (1855) [fig. 22], a picture of a man pouring a basket of potatoes into a sack held open by a woman. Again, by turning their faces away from the spectator, Millet down-

played the personalities of his anonymous peasants and focused all attention on the performance of their tasks. Most likely inspired by this work, Breton exhibited his own version of the subject a year later at the Salon [fig. 23]. In this interpretation he eliminates all but the two central figures, who now are enlarged to fill almost the entire space of the canvas. By silhouetting their compact, simplified forms against a light sky and a low, featureless horizon, Breton created an image of a labor as clearly delineated and emblematic as an antique cameo. His preliminary sketch of the scene, closer than his finished canvas to Millet's picture, makes evident Breton's conscious choices in the evolution of the theme. Progressing from the sketch to the Salon work, Breton lowered the horizon, thereby better distinguishing the figures from the dark mass of the background. The lower

Fig. 23. Jules Breton, *The Potato Harvest,* 1868, oil on canvas, 49¾ × 41¼ in.
The Pennsylvania Academy of the Fine Arts, Bequest of Henry C. Gibson.

horizon line places the spectator's vantage point somewhat below the level of the figures, conferring on them a monumentality and nobility consonant with the artist's idealized view of the French peasantry.

The marked differences between the two leading interpreters of rural life, Breton and Millet, were best summed up in their time by Thoré in his appraisal of the 1867 Universal Exposition.

> All that is called "grand painting," is banal and insignificant. . . . Millet and Breton seem to us the two artists who stand out immediately. Very different from one another, although they are attached to similar subjects, to the expression of rustic life, Millet brings to it a melancholy austerity, and what is striking in his peasantries, is the harshness of a work without respite and almost without recompense. Breton shows rather the celebration of work in open air, with its wholesome gaiety and even its elegance. The peasants of Millet are still serfs dominated by a sort of longstanding fatality; those of Breton feel themselves emancipated and take pleasure in their rural function. Utility and pleasure are, in effect, the two extremes of a rustic poem. Millet makes us think: "Wait. These people who produce everything do not look so happy, and this digger has much pain." Breton: "Ah! But how good the fields smell just after the hay is cut, and these haymakers are better off there than in an industrial workshop or in a bourgeois drawing room."[35]

Breton continued his monumentalization of peasant women into the years of the Third Republic. In the politically charged climate following France's defeat in the Franco-Prussian War, his work can be seen as a conscious striving to transform peasants into symbols of national strength. In reference to one of Breton's images, a pious Brittany girl carrying a rosary and candle, in 1873 the critic Castagnary observed: "Isn't it already a great sign of democratic progress to see a painter take a peasant for a model and by the force of style as well as the elevation of sentiment make of it the characteristic representation of an entire race? There is in this idea the stamp of the Republic of 1870."[36] At this time Breton concentrated on single images of standing peasant women whose coarse grandeur looked back to Delacroix's allegorical figure of Liberty (*Liberty Leading the People*, 1830), who was described in her day as a "strange blending of Phryne, fishwife, and goddess."[37] A drawing such as Breton's *Peasant Woman* [fig. 24], with her dominating presence and fierce pride, becomes a forceful symbol.

The culmination of this monumental treatment of the peasant was Breton's life-size *Gleaner* [fig. 25] exhibited at the Salon of 1877. Against the evening sky, a solitary gleaner bears a sheaf of grain in an image that has much in common with an earlier drawing by Millet, although Breton has aggrandized his figure into a heroine of epic stature by shifting the scale and emphasizing her proud features. Known as *La Glorieuse*, the painting was bought by the State for the Luxembourg Museum and was praised by orthodox contemporary critics. The New York reviewer for the *Art Journal* wrote: "No sentimental, soft-eyed damsel is this, like the fishergirls of Merle, but a rustic Juno, strong-armed, large eyed, and massively built, a very daughter of the field. She is a grand-looking creature, but withal a peasant and a toiler of the land."[38] According to Henry Houssaye, who thought the work merited the Medal of Honor at the Salon, "Breton showed us the peasant in his general character. He saw the prototype of the species through the individual. Certainly we never encountered a peasant like the *Gleaner*, but never did a peasant give us so vital and penetrating an impression."[39] Charles Bigot declared: "All the poetry of the harvest, all the strength of our industrious and honest race of the North is in this watchful peasant, in

Fig. 24. Jules Breton, *Peasant Woman*, pencil on paper, 15 × 10½ in. Musée des Beaux-Arts, Bordeaux.

Fig. 25. Jules Breton, *The Gleaner,* 1877, oil on canvas. Musée des Beaux-Arts, Arras.

this rustic Ceres, imitated not from the antique, but nature herself."[40] The grandeur of Breton's great gleaner —the noble peasant image—embodied for his contemporaries their aspirations for an archetypal image of the soul of France.

Notes

1. Eugene Bonnemère, *Histoire des paysans depuis la fin du Moyen-Age jusqu'à nos jours, 1200-1850* (Paris, 1856).

2. For an overview of nineteenth-century French peasants, see particularly Eugen Weber, *Peasants into Frenchmen: The Modernization of Rural France, 1870-1914* (Stanford, Calif., 1976).

3. J. D. Macmillan offers a full discussion on the relationship of this work to Boucher in "Holman Hunt's Hireling Shepherd: some reflections on a Victorian pastoral," *Art Bulletin* 54 (June 1972):187-97.

4. Robert Herbert presents this case in "City vs. Country: The Rural Image in French Painting from Millet to Gauguin," *Artforum* 8 (February 1970):44-45.

5. Jules Breton, *La Vie d'un Artiste: Art et Nature* (Paris, 1890), pp. 244-45, and Breton, *Un Peintre paysan: Souvenirs & Impressions* (Paris, 1896), pp. 122-23. For an expanded discussion of the work, see Gabriel P. Weisberg with Annette Bourrut-Lacouture, "Jules Breton's 'The Grape Harvest at Château-Lagrange,'" *Arts Magazine* 55 (January 1981): 98-103.

6. Breton, *Un Peintre paysan*, p. 122.

7. Weisberg and Bourrut-Lacouture, p. 100.

8. Breton, *Un Peintre paysan*, p. 121.

9. Breton, *La Vie d'un Artiste*, pp. 184-85.

10. Critic for the *Correspondent*, 29 July 1831, cited by Nicos Hadjinicolaou, "L'Exigence de 'réalisme' au Salon de 1831," *Histoire et critique des arts* 4-5 (May 1978):30.

11. Breton, *La Vie d'un Artiste*, p. 177, trans. Linda Nochlin, *Realism* (Middlesex, England, 1971), p. 113.

12. Breton, *La Vie d'un Artiste*, pp. 219-22.

13. Breton, *Un Peintre paysan*, pp. 44-45.

14. Alain Morel, "Power and Ideology in the Village Community of Picardy: Past and Present," in *Rural Society in France: Selections from the Annales Economies, Sociétés, Civilisations*, ed. Robert Forster and Orest Ranum, trans. Elborg Forster and Patricia M. Ranum (Baltimore, 1977), p. 108.

15. Ibid., p. 116.

16. Ibid.

17. Ibid.

18. Breton, *Un Peintre paysan*, pp. 83-84.

19. Ibid., p. 104.

20. Madeleine Fidell-Beaufort, *"Fire in a Haystack* by Jules Breton," *Bulletin of the Detroit Institute of Arts* 57, no. 2 (1979):61.

21. *The Recall of the Gleaners* was purchased by Napoleon III at the Salon for 8,000 francs and was given to the Luxembourg Museum in 1862.

22. Henri Delaborde, "L'Art français au Salon de 1859," *Revue des deux mondes*, 2nd ser., 21 (1 June 1859):512.

23. Alexandre Dumas, *L'Art et les artistes contemporains au Salon de 1859* (Paris, 1859), pp. 51-53.

24. Cited by Eugène Montrosier, *Les Artistes modernes*, 4 vols. (Paris, 1881-84), 3:51.

25. Paul Mantz, "Salon de 1859," *Gazette des Beaux-Arts* 2 (June 1859):287.

26. Of *Wine Shop—Monday*, Mantz noted that "Breton did not have the temperament of Brouwer or Ostade, and his rather thin painting only reveals here flat village caricatures," ibid., p. 286. Dumas found the work "vulgar" and "lacking distinction" and wrote that "Breton allowed himself to be tugged from below," *L'Art et les artistes contemporains*, p. 54. Zacharie Astruc faulted Breton's too-timid execution: "Such a scene, to be justified, required extraordinary brushwork." *Les 14 stations du Salon, 1859, suivies d'un recit douloureux* (Paris, 1859), pp. 230-31. On the other hand, five years later Jules-Antoine Castagnary could compliment the work as a "study of a vigorous reality." *Salons 1857-1870*, 2 vols. (Paris, 1892), 1:194.

27. Weisberg, *The Realist Tradition: French Painting and Drawing, 1830-1900*, exhibition catalogue (Cleveland: The Cleveland Museum of Art, 1980), p. 86.

28. In 1864 Thoré wrote: "Without metamorphosing a vineyard worker into an Erigone or a harvester into a Ceres,... M. Breton chooses his world, arranges it a little, conforms it—without deforming it—to certain standards of taste, washes it of original sin, and communicates to it his sentiment of fraternity and of progress; so well that his peasants no longer appear to be outside of current society. Is this what one calls the ideal? So much the better." Théophile Thoré [W. Bürger], *Salons de W. Bürger 1861 à 1868*, 2 vols. (Paris, 1870), 2:92-93. In 1865 Maxime du Camp noted: "The peasants of Breton are real peasants, even though they have a grandiose style that makes them admirable personages. In spite of their reality, they are epic, and one feels in seeing them that their task is as grand and as noble as anyone else's. In effect, today they are not only men, they are equals, and it is thus that M. Breton understands them." *Les Beaux Arts à l'Exposition universelle et aux Salons de 1863, 1864, 1865, 1866 et 1867* (Paris, 1867), p. 164.

29. Alfred Sensier and Mantz, *Jean François Millet, peasant and painter*, trans. de Kay (Boston, 1881), p. 93.

30. Ibid.

31. Théophile Gautier, "Salon de 1865," *Le Moniteur universelle*, 16 July 1865.

32. Mantz concluded his discussion by remarking that *"Close of the Day* is perhaps, among the works that M. Breton has shown us up to the present, the most complete and, in its apparent calm, the most moving." "Salon de 1865," *Gazette des Beaux-Arts* 18 (June 1865):518.

33. Thoré, p. 186.

34. Gautier's comment is in reference to Millet's *Winnower* at the Revolutionary 1848 Salon; cited by André Fermigier, *Jean-François Millet*, trans. Dinah Harrison (Geneva, 1977), p. 41.

35. Thoré, p. 361.

36. Castagnary, *Salons 1857-1870*, 2:60-61.

37. Heinrich Heine, *The Works of Heinrich Heine, The Salon* (London, 1893), p. 24, cited by Lorenz Eitner, *Neoclassicism and Romanticism 1750-1850, Sources and Documents*, 2 vols. (Englewood Cliffs, New Jersey, 1970), 2:152.

38. Lucy Hooper, "The Paris Salon of 1877-II," *The Art Journal* 3 (1877):250.

39. "Le Salon de 1882," *Revue des deux mondes*, 3rd ser., 51 (1 June 1882):584.

40. "La Peinture française en 1877," *Revue politique et littéraire* 19 (1877):1085.

Fig. 26. Léopold Robert, *The Arrival of the Harvesters in the Pontine Marshes,* 1830, oil on canvas, 56 × 83½ in. Musée du Louvre, Paris.

Jules Breton, Léopold Robert, and the Poetic Vision of Rural Life

by Gabriel P. Weisberg

ONE of the fundamental questions that arises when studying nineteenth-century painters closely associated with the academic tradition and popular taste of the period is the consideration of how artists developed their imagery and from what sources they often derived their compositions. Crucial to the investigation of these problems is the debt that many artists owed to painters of former times and the not-so-distant early years of the nineteenth century. It was by assessing and reusing the past—by trying to understand which earlier artists held a special meaning for painters of the present—that a painter such as Jules Breton continued the past into the present within a new guise.[1]

At the center of this process was the way in which artists learned to utilize motifs from painters of the past for their own compositions. By studying examples from previous periods in the academic ateliers in which they were trained, and by visiting public and private collections where they could actually study paintings from the past, younger artists developed a keen visual awareness of past traditions. Some copied artists by preparing studies in museums, such as the Louvre, that transcribed the compositions of painters from the Renaissance or the seventeenth century. Others were subtler in the ways in which they used the past, finding confirmation for their own theories in older modes of expression. Jules Breton, aside from receiving a standard academic training in technique, familiarized himself with the older masters; by following this tradition, he allied himself with a theory that saw little necessity in continually trying to invent new or even original modes of expression. In examining painters such as Nicolas Poussin or Leonardo da Vinci (artists Breton listed as major influences on his career in a published document), or relatively contemporary artists such as Léopold Robert, Breton apprenticed himself to painters who could help him develop his own style and personal point of view.[2] Since Robert was one of the most important younger romantic painters, his effect on the career and imagery of Breton is worth studying at some length. Indeed, Robert's fascination with rural themes may have been one of the reasons Breton cultivated the rural vision in his own work and hence is paramount to a fuller understanding of it.

Breton and Robert

As early as 1859, Jules Breton was identified by an art critic as the reincarnation of Léopold Robert, this comment revealing a growing recognition that a complex relationship existed between the young painter of rural themes and his romantic predecessor.[3] Breton was open in his declaration of admiration for Robert in his well-known volume *La Vie d'un Artiste,* exclaiming how Robert's *The Arrival of the Harvesters in the Pontine Marshes* [fig. 26], exhibited at the Louvre, had stimulated his imagination and how he had found it a significant composition for study.[4]

Although Breton was open in his admiration for Robert, the depth of his commitment to the Swiss painter has gone largely unexplored, even in the catalogue of the recent exhibition on Breton's career.[5] One of the dominant painters of the second generation of the romantic classical movement, Robert's career ended

Fig. 27. Emille Lassalle, *Lithographic Detail after "The Harvesters,"* c. 1843. Bibliothèque Nationale, Paris.

tragically with his suicide in 1835. Because his death came abruptly, at the apex of his brilliant career, Robert became a much-discussed artist, whose personality overshadowed his contribution to nineteenth-century art.[6] The curious aspect of Breton's grasp of Robert's significance, however, is that he was not overwhelmed by the artist's mystique. Instead, Robert, through his compositions and theories, became a visual model for some of Breton's rustic themes.

General admiration for Robert was widespread, reinforced by an intense cult that attracted writers, collectors, colleagues, and the general public. Aided by exhibition of Robert's canvases, by constant attention in the daily press, and by a far-reaching dissemination of his images through lithographic reproduction and by numerous copies, public and artistic awareness of Robert's contribution to nineteenth-century art escalated. His paintings were not hidden away for a small

band of connoisseurs; after his death his work entered a phase of public acclaim and examination. In order to grasp how and why Breton utilized Robert's ideas, it is essential to examine the appreciative trend generated for this romantic artist during the 1840s.

The Léopold Robert Cult

Following Robert's death in 1835, a strong interest in his work evolved from the myth of his personality and from extensive rumors of his melancholy existence. Some writers tried to romanticize his career by emphasizing the loneliness of his life. Others were inspired by Robert's personal vision of the Italian peasant, a viewpoint that combined a romantic love of the exotic (color and dress) with a classical interest in linearity and idealization. These qualities were further enhanced by the exhibition of certain canvases in France, including *The*

Arrival of the Harvesters, which was eventually exhibited in the Luxembourg Museum, where it was admired by generations of painters.

Robert's vision of Italian peasant types was made known by the dissemination of numerous lithographs after his compositions, images which began appearing by the mid 1840s. Whether details from *The Harvesters* [figs. 27 and 28] or examples of other peasant types, these images underscored Robert's sentimental attachment to the rustic poor who had been either jeopardized by natural disaster or seriously affected by a life of hardship and travail. While lithographs were widely distributed, watercolor copies were also widespread, adding to the increased exposure of Robert's work.

Robert's peasants carried themselves with a sense of personal dignity, a grandeur which conveyed an aura of magnanimity in the face of personal calamity. Even when a figure gave vent to outright passion or despair, emotions were held in control, as if classical stoicism prevented Robert from going to extremes. In effect, his sense of understatement became one of the leitmotifs of

Fig. 28. Emille Lassalle, *Lithographic Detail after "The Harvesters",* c. 1844. Bibliothèque Nationale, Paris.

his style; it was this quality, among others, that was transmitted to Jules Breton and which appeared in a number of his figures.

By 1848, at the moment Breton was preparing his first major Salon canvas, *Want and Despair,* his attention was undoubtedly drawn to Robert by the publication of a long essay on the painter in the widely read *Revue des deux mondes.*[7] This three-part article is worth examining at some length, since it provides further clues to the fascination with Robert at this particular moment in history, and because it offers some reasons why Robert's style was attracting a growing audience.

If there was a sense of frustration, of sadness, that hovered over Robert's brief career because of his suicide, writers also recognized a seriousness to his work that was wedded with a *sentiment religieux.*[8] Robert's determination to create dignified scenes from obvious peasant misery, to see something real and positive in the world he was capturing on canvas, suggested that he was trying to move away from latent romantic issues toward a *"vivante réalité."* Here scenes and types from society were being used for a higher purpose, to suggest an *"idée actuelle."*[9] Robert's ability to transcend the mundane, to find aspects of nobility in the face of the common fisherman or field laborer, created an impression of beatitude in his studies of the humble and the poor. This attitude, as underscored by some writers, went far toward imbuing his art with exceptionally high-minded principles, those virtues that were also instilled in Breton through the teachings of his family, especially that of his Uncle Boniface.[10]

There were other reasons why Robert was then being highly regarded. In the mid 1830s, critic Achille Allier tried to create a center for the study of French provincial life in Moulins through the organization of exhibitions that had an impact on community life and the publication of a journal.[11] He emphasized the need for artists to seek broad inspiration. In his advocacy of rural life, he used Robert as a paramount example of a painter who focused on provincial (albeit Italian) types, such as harvesters and haygatherers. Although Allier died at an early age, the movement he helped initiate, through a focus on rustic life, continued. This may have been another clear reason why Breton found the work of Robert part of a new, compelling tradition.

Robert was also significant for another reason. His best known canvases, such as *The Harvesters,* showed a mastery of past and current painters. His ability to understand, and to utilize, the compositions of Raphael, as in a series of independent studies of peasants, recreated in

Fig. 29. Emille Lassalle, *Italian Woman Weeping Over the Ruins,* after Léopold Robert, 1844. Bibliothèque Nationale, Paris.

the faces of rural maidens a sense of Italian Renaissance beauty and innocence and demonstrated how the past could be kept alive and could be reinterpreted. This stylistic attitude, united with Robert's interest in episodes from peasant life—through his determination to see the seasons in new guises—earned him support from Breton and the critics of 1848.

Breton and Léopold Robert in Context

As a young student in Belgium during the 1840s and later as a member of Martin Drolling's atelier in Paris, Breton would have found favor for his predilection for the works of Léopold Robert. The Swiss artist was continually being extolled as a model for young Belgian artists by art critics who reviewed the annual exhibitions in either Antwerp or Ghent. Clearly Robert's *Harvesters,* noted by these writers, was emulated by other younger Belgian painters in rural peasant themes of their own.[12] *The Harvesters* was seen as Robert's unparalleled master-

piece, the canvas which crowned his career and the painting by which his influence on young artists, both in the Low Countries and in France, could best be discerned. Before his death Robert had worked on a replica of the composition, since it had been demanded by private collectors;[13] its eventual exhibition at the Louvre made the original canvas a highly visible work which appealed to younger artists eager to unite the real and the ideal in rustic peasant scenes.

Robert was known not only by *The Harvesters;* several of his paintings were found in provincial French museums, suggesting that there was a ready audience and market for his compositions in the rural regions of the country. As early as 1860, the Nantes museum exhibited canvases from the late 1820s; other compositions of young peasant girls were owned by private collectors and discussed in the *Gazette des Beaux-Arts* (1872).[14] This, then, records the continuing interest in Robert's compositions well after his death as part of the constant fascination with rural life.

Periodically, Breton commented on how Robert had been a guiding force in his career. He noted in *Nos Peintres du siècle* how he had studied *The Harvesters* first in the Luxembourg Museum, as the young artist justly believed Robert had been properly glorified for realizing the public taste of the period. It is this concept that seems quite central to the way Robert was viewed by collectors eager to have paintings that mirrored the increasing sentiment in rustic life; it is also this quality which was found in Breton, who was often seen as mirroring

Although *The Harvesters* occupied a central place in Breton's admiration for Robert, it was not the only canvas or theme that Breton utilized. The Swiss painter was well known for creating studies of beautiful rural maidens [fig. 29] or scenes of a mother and child [fig. 30] which appealed to collectors and younger artists. If Breton seldom focused on these themes alone, he did manage to create family groups—often with a mother and child in an open field—that suggested very strong Biblical parallels [fig. 31]. That inspiration for this theme came solely from Robert is doubtful, since it was a motif widely used by other romantic and academic painters; but what often seems most striking in Breton's imagery is the sense of tranquility, the sort of repose which Robert had captured in his work. Beyond this, Breton's sense of melancholy detachment may also be attributable to the way in which Robert depicted his models to create a highly dignified scene.

Though his works were often thought to be too idealized, a few critics did understand what Breton was trying to do. Some eulogized him for being simpler and truer than Robert, and there were others, such as Paul Mantz, who in 1878 sounded a note of caution for the painter. He wanted to see Breton move away from his dependency on the idealization inherent in a study of Robert toward a new sense of naturalism, as in Breton's painting *The Siesta*. Mantz wanted Breton's figures to reflect an ease of pose, a heightened truthfulness and a firmer grasp of reality from observable life.[15] Thus, in discussing Breton's interest in Robert, it is essential to see that some subtle changes were taking place in the artist in response to social pressures. It is also necessary to analyze the impact of Robert with considerable caution, since it was not always the same type of involvement at given moments in Breton's career.

Breton's Use of Robert

Perhaps the first strong echo of the works of Léopold Robert was found in Breton's 1853 Salon canvas, *Return*

Fig. 30. Emille Lassalle, *Lithographic Detail after "The Harvesters",* c. 1843. Bibliothèque Nationale, Paris.

Fig. 31. Jules Breton, *Two Peasants Resting,* chalk on paper, 24 × 18 in. Brandt Dayton, New York.

Fig. 32. Jules Breton, *The Return of the Harvesters,* 1853, oil on canvas. Private collection, Belgium.

of the Harvesters [fig. 32], a work too often maligned as being overly contrived when, in reality, it must be seen as a pioneering effort in Breton's attempt to examine peasant and rustic themes. If the sense of robust carousing, rollicking fun was utilized by Breton to demonstrate peasants rejoicing at the close of their harvest, certain figures in the composition, and the way they were situated, clearly suggest how Breton tried to assimilate aspects of Robert's style while maintaining the reality of his theme.

The most apparent relationship with Robert's canvas is in the pose of the male figure at the right of the *Return*. His dance with a female partner underscores the merriment associated with the termination of the harvest; his movements suggest once again how Breton assimilated the two male figures in Robert's work (one with a bagpipe) to create one form that symbolizes dance. Simi-

larly, the way in which the man and woman move into the scene at the left, with the woman holding a bundle of hay, recalls the placement of the two women to the left of Robert's canvas. Other than these visual parallels, however, Breton's version of field harvesting is free of heavy dependency on his predecessor. In this early canvas Breton emphasized a type of semi-anecdotal painting uniting references to past masters (i.e., Poussin or painters of the Italian Renaissance) with an earthy strain to capture what he regarded as joyous celebration of the cessation of field labor.

If *Return of the Harvesters* did not bring Breton the public recognition he hoped for (not until the 1855 Salon did he obtain a medal), the painting did propel him toward consideration of all aspects of rural life and labor. Breton increasingly recorded rural energies (i.e., *Fire in a Haystack*), as well as seasonal activities, in an effort to combine the real with the ideal, to create a stately vision of peasant life in keeping with what had been advocated by certain governmental officials of the Second Empire.[16]

Perhaps few other works by Breton, beyond a drawing of a young mother and her child in the fields titled *Two Peasants Resting* [fig. 31], demonstrate the link with Robert's beatific personifications. In the drawing, Breton's emphasis is on a quality of sentiment suffused with an inner strength that creates a mood of pious solemnity. It leads one directly away from the overly mundane toward the creation of a higher reality, a higher realm of existence. Breton has mastered, in this extremely subtle and nuanced work, Robert's ability to show nobility in the humblest, most common theme drawn from the life of the fields. Like Millet in *The Angelus* [fig. 54], he has created a distinct impression of holy beatitude—similar to an Italian Renaissance Madonna and Child—underscoring an appealing sentiment for one to find, or associate with, in the workers of the field. In a sense, Breton has deliberately cleansed his laborers of any ''ugly'' qualities, removed the impression of dirt or grime, and has made his figures both handsome and beautiful. But beauty to Breton seemed a virtue and not a sin; by bringing his field types close to a viewer, he created a virtuous mood that reached outwards.

It is difficult to pinpoint the exact date for the creation of this drawing, however, during the late 1850s (the logical moment for its completion) Breton did a series of realistic scenes depicting activities and popular types from rural villages. These gradually changed his style in accordance with his vision of a stately romantic-classicism initiated by Robert. Thus, the graceful rhythms inherent in Breton's 1859 *Recall of the Gleaners* [fig. 33] suggests the movement of Italian Renaissance compositions, while the figural types and facial features that Breton gave his models suggest the dignity and nobility of Robert's best peasant types. This direction became even more highly developed in Breton's works of the early 1860s for independent patrons.

By 1862, under commission from the wealthy Comte Duchâtel, Breton traveled to Château Lagrange, near Bordeaux, to begin studies for a work that would focus on the annual grape harvest on the Duchâtel estate. While there, Breton completed a number of preliminary drawings, watercolors, and oil sketches in preparation for a canvas he finished in Courrières and which he eventually exhibited at the 1864 Paris Salon. If the painting evolved from a realist study of actual workers in the field, as well as from a sense of acute observation, the final version emerged as a clear integration of the real and the ideal.

Robert's *Arrival of the Harvesters* is also apparent in *The Vintage at Château Lagrange* [fig. 7]. While Breton moved the oxcart from the center of Robert's composition to the periphery, the presence of this rustic vehicle and its role in gathering and holding the grapes is para-

Fig. 33. Jules Breton, *The Recall of the Gleaners,* 1859, oil on canvas, 35⅞ × 69⅞ in. Musée des Beaux-Arts, Arras.

Fig. 34. Jules Breton, *Evening,* 1860, oil on canvas. Musée du Louvre, Paris.

mount. Most importantly, and aside from the friezelike arrangement of the figures across the frontal plane (another similarity with *The Harvesters*), Breton's central women move according to stately rhythms, in a balanced, ordered way suggestive of the manner in which Robert situated his elegant Italian peasants to the left of the painting. The serene cast to the facial features and their slightly dreamy expressions may also have been due to his assimilation of Robert's mood of classical idealism. Certainly the necessity of capturing a southern type, a Bordelais, to use the terminology of the period, may also have led Breton toward further study of Robert's women. His idealized Italian women could be seen as models of the type advocated by Comte Duchâtel as part of the reality he wanted for his composition.[17] The issue of whether Breton worked from photographs to capture the nuances of pose and demeanor,

as has been recorded in family letters, seems secondary to his increasing awareness of the need to temper harsh reality for the Salon.

The influence of Robert may also be seen in other works that Breton completed in the 1860s, such as *Evening* [fig. 34], where the solitary figure, positioned close to the frontal plane of the composition, stares off into space. This was not a new arrangement, but it differed in that the contemplative pose of the figure was sharply contrasted with the reality of locale and detail of dress.[18] In creating this scheme, Breton may have had in mind other works by Robert, where a solitary figure was placed in a contemplative pose looking out on the Mediterranean Sea [fig. 35]. In situating his figure close to the frontal plane, by revealing one foot, and by using an asymmetrical balance, Robert provided motifs that Breton could assimilate for his own purposes. In addition, Robert's sense of stoic grace, serenity, and meditative calm were used by Breton to create a harmonious relationship between form and content.

Thus, the importance of Léopold Robert as a model continued throughout Breton's career. Breton may have been reinforced in this predilection by the appearance of Charles Clément's *Léopold Robert, d'après sa correspondance* (1875), which provided an intimate glimpse of the painter's personal life and career. This volume underscored the subtle relationship between reality and poetry that marked much of Robert's own work and his ability to imbue his peasants with a strong sense of sincerity.

In this way, Breton found continued reinforcement for his personal, poetic vision of rustic life. The pensive mood of the field laborers, their melancholy attitude,

was partly motivated by Robert's earlier examples. When Breton painted a peasant staring into space, he also reiterated the sense of escape that Robert had revealed. In Breton's mature compositions, he increasingly eliminated the ugliness of much rural existence to create a genuinely idyllic mood. In a sense, Breton created a higher reality where peasants worked with timeless dignity and purpose. If Breton's view of peasant life was at variance with reality and did not reflect the crises of the day in industrialization or rural depopulation, his rustic models were conditioned by his idolatry of earlier masters. Robert, with his classical resolve to see rustic life as linked to older traditions, helped Breton create a world largely untouched by modern anxiety, a realm filled with idealized poetic innocence. In a sense, he helped Breton visualize the theory of the use of past masters as models

Fig. 35. Léopold Robert, *Young Girl of Capri,* 1826, oil on canvas. Musée d'Art et d'Histoire, Geneva.

for a new artistic vision, thereby making it less necessary to condemn Breton for taking too few risks or for being too conventional, as some still do. It is thus all the more essential to see and understand the alternative context in which he was working. Breton now appears as a master of a mode of creativity based on past traditions becoming relevant again for the present.

Notes

1. Much of French painting during the Second Empire has been seen within the context of past styles becoming relevant for the present, as articulated in Joseph C. Sloane, *French Painting Between the Past and the Present: Artists, Critics and Traditions from 1848 to 1870* (Princeton: Princeton University Press, 1951). While Sloane used Jules Breton as a convenient foil against which the evolution of modernism could be discerned, Sloane suggested there were traditions in French art of the time that were deeply ingrained in the French psyche and which were very apparent in the work of some painters of the period. Sloane identified an alternative method of creativity, based largely on academic methods, which emerged from a world of ideas and traditions linked to the eighteenth century and the continuation of history painting as a pretext for artistic imagery. Breton clearly relates to this group. His dependency on earlier modes of visual expression can be explained by this contextualization.

Despite this way of reading Breton's work, and without overemphasizing his type of realism (especially noticeable in several of his earliest canvases), some art historians persist in negating Breton's contributions by citing his failure to be modern. This attitude, partially constructed by Sloane, was utilized by Linda Nochlin in her examination of Breton within the context of *The Realist Tradition* exhibition. See Linda Nochlin, "The Realist Tradition: French Painting and Drawing 1830-1910," *Burlington Magazine* 123 (April 1981):263-69. Others, such as Eunice Lipton, continue to see Breton as a foil for the modernist position without fully recognizing the complexity of this alternative way of creating or understanding how central it was to artists in the nineteenth century.

2. Breton never disguised his admiration for a number of old masters, talking freely about his tastes in many of his publications. Discussions with artistic colleagues also would have disclosed these predilections most clearly. However, in a brief synopsis of his career, published within his lifetime, Breton made very specific reference to key aspects of his personal concepts. It would have been quite easy for readers of this document and artistic colleagues of the time to know into which camp his sympathies fully belonged. For further reference, see "Les Confidences de Salon—Jules Breton," *Revue illustrée* 15 (December 1892—June 1893):252.

3. The relationship between Breton and Léopold Robert was noticed by several nineteenth-century critics. Among the first was Henri Delaborde, "L'Art français au Salon de 1859," *Revue des deux mondes* 21 (May—June 1859):512, who wrote, "M. Breton est-il appelé à devenir le Léopold Robert de nos campagnes. C'est la une belle place à prendre: puisse-t-il se rendre tout à fait digne de l'occuper!" In a sense, Breton's relationship with Robert could be compared with a number of still-life painters (Bonvin, Ribot, Vollon) who were continually being compared with Chardin. Both these cases were meant as compliments to demonstrate in which tradition certain nineteenth-century painters were working and how their canvases could be favorably compared with the leading past masters. Viewing their work in this light negates the necessity of seeing a direct confrontation with tendencies that the twentieth century has interpreted as being solely modernist.

4. For reference, see Jules Breton, *La Vie d'un Artiste* (Paris, 1896), p. 152. In this reference Breton suggests that he had seen Robert's compositions in official Parisian museums. It is possible, although not fully documented, that works by Robert would have been available for artists to see in several leading private collections.

5. For further reference, see Gabriel P. Weisberg, "Jules Breton in Context," *Jules Breton and the French Rural Tradition*, exhibition catalogue (Omaha, Neb.: Joslyn Art Museum, 1982). Aside from a passing reference to Robert in Breton's writings, the author has not located a study that outlines the relationship between both painters. For further reference to Robert's career, see E. Manganel, "Léopold Robert," *Beaux-Arts* 139 (30 August 1938):1, 6.

6. For a discussion of Robert's personality and career published shortly after his death, see E. J. Delecluze, *Notice sur la vie et les ouvrages de Léopold Robert* (Paris: Rittner et Goupil, Editeurs, 1838).

7. For reference see F. Feuillet de Conches, "Peintres et Sculpteurs Modernes—Léopold Robert," *Revue des deux mondes* (July/September 1848):887-913; ibid (October/December 1848):32-70, 353-95. This important article provides a comprehensive view of Robert's contribution to nineteenth-century art drawn from a series of unpublished letters and documents. The fact that this article was prepared at all suggests a very strong prevailing interest in presenting Robert in a detailed way at this moment in time. The audience that read this particular series of articles was probably extensive, providing yet another barometer of the importance of Robert's work to many and the necessity for other artists to learn and absorb what he had accomplished.

8. Ibid, p. 354. This attitude was especially noticeable in Robert's *Pêcheurs de l'Adriatique* exhibited at the 1836 Paris Salon.

9. Ibid. This was one of the persistent concepts of Robert's work. By working in this particular vein, Robert was seen as preparing the idea first, conceptualizing his theme, and then as proceeding to develop a number of preparatory sketches where the idea was visualized. This method of working may have allowed for a large effect of originality, one of the major qualities noticed by the critics when they reviewed Robert's compositions.

10. For further information on the teachings and relationship between Jules Breton and his Uncle Boniface, see Annette Bourrut-Lacouture, "The Origins and Youth of Jules Breton," in *Jules Breton and the French Rural Tradition*, pp. 29-36. Bourrut-Lacouture is preparing an extensive monograph on Breton.

11. For reference to the importance of Achille Allier in promoting a strong cult of rural life, see Léon Rosenthal, *Du Romantisme au réalisme* (Paris, 1914), pp. 71-72.

12. Robert had a very marked impact on the Davidian followers in Belgium and on the methods of teaching art in the art schools. During the 1840s those artists who completed rustic themes were often compared with Robert, who was then regarded as the primary figure to invest such themes with importance and whose compositions had a high level of quality. For further reference to this attitude, see "Exposition des Beaux-Arts à Anvers," *L'Illustration* (24 October 1846):123-26.

13. For reference to a "répétition" of *The Harvesters*, see de Conches, "Peintres," p. 394. This example apparently was not fully completed for Count Raczynski in Berlin, although the fact that Robert had been asked to complete another version of this famous work demonstrates how far afield he was known and appreciated and in which circles he moved. It is unknown whether Robert did any other copies of this particular composition.

14. For further reference see Olivier Merson, "Musées de Province, La Galerie Clarke de Feltre, Musée de Nantes," *Gazette des Beaux-Arts* 8 (1860):197-202; and Paul Mantz, "La Galerie de M. Maurice Cottier," *Gazette des Beaux-Arts* 30 (1872):375ff.

15. Mantz, "Exposition Universelle de 1878: La Peinture française," *Gazette des Beaux-Arts* 18 (October 1878):436.

16. See Albert Boime, "The Second Empire's Official Realism," in *The European Realist Tradition*, ed. Weisberg (Bloomington: Indiana University Press, 1982), pp. 31-123.

17. See Weisberg with Bourrut-Lacouture, "Jules Breton's 'The Grape Harvest at Château-Lagrange,'" *Arts Magazine* 55 (January 1981):100ff.

18. For another work, *Rest*, in a similar guise, see *The Second Empire, Art in France under Napoleon III*, exhibition catalogue (Philadelphia: Philadelphia Museum of Art, 1978), p. 261.

Willa Cather and the French Rural Tradition of Breton and Millet

O Pioneers!, The Song of the Lark, and *My Ántonia*

by Susan J. Rosowski

RADICAL change presents to artists the challenge of new subjects and ideas. This was the case in nineteenth-century France when, following the 1830 Revolution, art critics, like liberal reformers, called for artists to paint regional French figures rather than traditional classical ones and to deal with contemporary life.[1] The French rural tradition was one response to this challenge, by which artists sought to bring art to their own country and neighborhood. Thus, Jules Breton used peasant subjects, dressing them in costumes depicted in realistic detail and placing them in settings of his own locale, and Jean-François Millet employed a monumental style to depict peasants at work.

It was a tradition of far-reaching influence, extending to the Nebraska writer Willa Cather. When she began to write at the turn of the twentieth century, Cather was facing an artistic challenge analogous to that which informed the French rural tradition—to break away from convention and to find her own voice. Like Breton and Millet, Cather would become best known for using her native region (i.e., the American Midwest and, particularly, Nebraska) for art of the highest order, with noble subjects and epic themes. And like them, she realized that doing so would involve a radical departure from tradition. Her Nebraska region, after all, was settled by immigrant Swedes, and "the Swede had never appeared on the printed page in this country except in broadly humorous sketches." And even more challenging, these Swedes were "heavy farming people, with cornfields and pasture lands and pig yards—set in Nebraska, of all places!"[2] Such was Willa Cather's own neighborhood, "as new, as unknown to art as it was to the pioneer."[3]

Cather's early writing tells of evading those native materials by following certain literary models, then coming to terms with them assisted by artistic ones. In literature she turned to Henry James, whom she called "the Master" and whose influence is evident in her highly conventional first novel, *Alexander's Bridge* (1912). In the same year that *Alexander's Bridge* was published, however, so was "The Bohemian Girl," a short story that tells of Cather's finding more suitable models in Dutch genre painting and the French rural tradition. Indeed, the weakest part of "The Bohemian Girl" is its most conventionally literary, i.e., its romantic, rather melodramatic plot. Nils Ericson returns to his boyhood Nebraska home, where he meets his childhood sweetheart, Clara Vavrika, now married to Nils's unimaginative older brother. Nils's and Clara's love rekindles, and together they flee from small-town life.

Against the background of a conventional plot flash brilliant descriptive scenes depicting the everyday life of immigrant farmers in her native Nebraska, and for them Cather consciously drew upon visual art.[4] As if putting down her pen and taking up a brush, Cather suspended action and plot to describe, for example, a dinner following a barn raising. Open barn doors frame an assembly of women, platters of food, and piles of melons, all rendered in rich detail:

Nils leaned against the booth, talking to the excited little girl and watching the people. The barn faced the west, and the sun, pouring in at the big doors, filled the whole interior with a golden light, through which filtered fine particles of dust from the haymow, where the children were romping. There was a great chattering from the stall where Johanna

Vavrika exhibited to the admiring women her platters heaped with fried chicken, her roasts of beef, boiled tongues, and baked hams with cloves stuck in the crisp brown fat and garnished with tansy and parsley. The older women, having assured themselves that there were twenty kinds of cake, not counting cookies, and three dozen fat pies, repaired to the corner behind the pile of watermelons, put on their white aprons, and fell to their knitting and fancywork. They were a fine company of old women, and *a Dutch painter would have loved to find them there together* [italics added], where the sun made bright patches on the floor and sent long, quivering shafts of gold through the dusky shade up among the rafters. There were fat, rosy old women who looked hot in their best dresses; spare, alert old women with brown, dark-veined hands; and several of almost heroic frame, not less massive than old Mrs. Ericson herself. Few of them wore glasses, and old Mrs. Svendsen, a Danish woman, who was quite bald, wore the only cap among them. Mrs. Oleson, who had twelve grandchildren, could still show two braids of yellow hair as thick as her own wrists. Among all these grandmothers there were more brown heads than white. They all had a pleased, prosperous air, as if they were more than satisfied with themselves and with life. Nils, leaning against Hilda's lemonade stand, watched them as they sat chattering in four languages, their fingers never lagging behind their tongues.

"Look at them over there," he whispered, detaining Clara as she passed him. "Aren't they the Old Guard? I've just counted thirty hands. I guess they've wrung many a chicken's neck and warmed many a boy's jacket for him in their time."

In reality he fell into amazement when he thought of the Herculean labors those fifteen pairs of hands had performed; of the cows they had milked, the butter they had made, the gardens they had planted, the children and grandchildren they had tended, the brooms they had worn out, the mountains of food they had cooked. It made him dizzy. [5]

The careful composition of this scene suggests a painting. The point of view is established by Nils, who directs attention to the central figure, Johanna Vavrika, exhibiting her platters of food. She is set against a background of admiring women brought to life by the detailing of their aprons, veined hands, braided hair, and the single cap. The company of women in the lower corner is balanced by the romping children in the haymow above. Sun pouring in the open doors of the barn provides warm light. As Cather recognized when she wrote "a Dutch painter would have loved to find them there," the scene is domestic and full in the manner of Dutch genre painting. Cather has added her own stamp, however, which distinguishes her treatment from that of Dutch art. This is a scene that strains against domesticity and toward the heroic, with the amassed "mountains" of food, the women who are "of almost heroic frame," and the "Herculean labors they have performed." It is a scene

that suggests Cather's receptivity to the French tradition that elevates rural subjects to noble proportions.

Cather had long felt strong ties to French culture. As her biographer James Woodress writes, "Willa Cather had been a Francophile from early childhood," an allegiance that intensified when in 1902 she spent six weeks in France and "at Barbizon, the locale of Millet, Rousseau, and others of the Barbizon' school."[6] Her respect for artists of the French rural tradition is evident in her essays and especially in her frequent references to Jules Breton and Jean-François Millet. Cather gave her highest praise to Millet, using him repeatedly as the major example of her belief that simplification is necessary for great art. *The Sower* [fig. 38] was preceded by hundreds of sketches of peasants sowing grain, Cather wrote, which Millet distilled into the one figure that preserved the spirit of the whole.[7]

Even as Cather was placing Millet in the highest ranks of art, she was writing of Breton with an enthusiasm that suggests a personal allegiance. Cather granted that Breton lacked the profundity and technique of Millet, but she defended his power and his place "in the catholic kingdom of art."[8] Cather especially praised Breton's power of teaching art to the untutored peoples of the prairies. In 1901 she wrote:

It is not unlikely that the Chicago Art Institute, with its splendid casts and pictures, has done more for the people of the Middle West than any of the city's great industries. Every farmer boy who goes into the city to order his stock, takes a look at the pictures. There are thousands of people all over the prairies who have seen their first and only good pictures there. They elect their favorites and go back to see them year after year. . . .You will find hundreds of merchants and farmer boys all over Nebraska and Kansas and Iowa who remember Jules Breton's beautiful "Song of the Lark," and perhaps the ugly little peasant girl standing barefoot among the wheat fields in the early morning has taught some of these people to hear the lark sing for themselves.[9]

Cather's predisposition to a French influence and to artists of the French rural tradition—especially to Breton and Millet—signals her own treatment of her native country. For it was the manner of Breton's *Song of the Lark* [fig. 36], with its treatment of a rural subject in an elevated style and a pastoral mood, combined with an appeal to the creative imagination in the manner of Millet, that Cather employed in *O Pioneers!,* the work in which she "hit the home pasture."[10]

Similarities between *O Pioneers!* and Breton's paintings are striking. In *O Pioneers!* Cather developed not a narrative line so much as a series of scenes, like paintings, presenting the immigrant pioneer, Alexandra Berg-

Fig. 36. Jules Breton, *The Song of the Lark,* 1884, oil on canvas, 43½ × 33¾ in. The Art Institute of Chicago, Henry Field Memorial Collection.

son. Much as Breton's peasants are noble of bearing, calm, in harmony with nature, so is Alexandra. She is often described by an onlooker who establishes a perspective that is upward and that supports his tone of admiration, respect, and awe. Her younger brother, for example, accompanying her as she climbs the Divide, describes her awakening to the beauty of her own region, her radiant face set toward the land "with love and yearning."[11] Similarly, Carl Linstrum, Alexandra's friend and future husband, comes upon her as she stands perfectly still amidst a garden, lost in thought, the sun highlighting her reddish hair. When alone, too, Alexandra is often posed motionless, gazing into the distance, as when she "stood leaning against the frame of the mill, looking at the stars which glittered so keenly through the frosty autumn air" (p. 70).

The novel is filled with such moments, conveyed by pictures in words. Like Breton's pictures set in his native Courrières, these scenes are drawn against a backdrop of Cather's own neighborhood of Red Cloud and the Divide, the high country in Webster County between the Republican and Little Blue rivers. Like Breton's paintings, they also are enriched by realistic detailing of food and dress. Cather writes that Alexandra's mother seasons her cherry preserves with lemon peel and that the hermit, Ivar, wears "a clean shirt of unbleached cotton, open at the neck" (pp. 29, 37). Most important, like Breton, Cather applies these realistic details to characters who seem types rather than individuals: in the opening scenes, Alexandra is above all "a fine human creature" (p. 8), her brother "a little country boy" (p. 5), and her mother "a good housewife" (p. 28). Characters' clothing tends to seem picturesque, unrelated to any activity. Alexandra often appears motionless, with her shawl about her and her sunbonnet or shade hat beside her, untouched by labor and aging. Her brothers do the work of taming the land offstage, while she provides the calm direction of a noble pioneering spirit. She is a pastoral figure who informs an idyll, a center of calm and repose. Even in years of drought, Alexandra seems remote from the worry and labor of the barren land, as if she is protected by a magical circle of fertility:

> The second of these barren summers was passing. One September afternoon Alexandra had gone over to the garden across the draw to dig sweet potatoes—they had been thriving upon the weather that was fatal to everything else. But when Carl Linstrum came up the garden rows to find her, she was not working. She was standing lost in thought, leaning upon her pitchfork, her sunbonnet lying beside her on the ground. The dry garden patch smelled of drying vines and was strewn with yellow seed cucumbers and pumpkins and citrons. At one end, next the rhubarb, grew feathery aspara-

gus, with red berries. Down the middle of the garden was a row of gooseberry and currant bushes. A few tough zenias [sic] and marigolds and a row of scarlet sage [were there]. . . .Carl came quietly and slowly up the garden path, looking intently at Alexandra. She did not hear him. She was standing perfectly still, with that serious ease so characteristic of her. Her thick, reddish braids, twisted about her head, fairly burned in the sunlight. (pp. 48-49)

Alexandra not only escapes time—she defies it. After sixteen years the land has changed dramatically, but "Alexandra herself has changed very little" (p. 87). Instead, unaltered by the coarsening effects of taming the land, she has become softer and more vital, for "her figure is fuller, and she has more color. She seems sunnier and more vigorous than she did as a young girl" (p. 87). Here, too, Cather uses secondary characters, especially Carl Linstrum, to provide a point of view and to paint a scene in words. And Cather gives Carl the qualifications to do so. He is an artist who, having left the region to acquire knowledge and skills in the larger world, can accurately interpret his native land and people upon his return. His descriptions are composed and picturesque, appropriate to the pastoral mood of the novel. He remembers, for example, Alexandra "when he saw her coming with her free step, her upright head and calm shoulders," and he interprets the scene by his feeling "that she looked as if she had walked straight out of the morning itself. Since then, when he had happened to see the sun come up on the country or on the water, he had often remembered the young Swedish girl and her milking pails" (p. 126). Later, when Carl sees Alexandra and her friend Marie in an orchard, he views the scene as a painting:

> Carl sat at a little distance from the two women, his back to the wheatfield, and watched them. Alexandra took off her shade-hat and threw it on the ground. Marie picked it up and played with the white ribbons, twisting them about her brown fingers as she talked. *They made a pretty picture* [italics added] in the strong sunlight, the leafy pattern surrounding them like a net; the Swedish woman so white and gold, kindly and amused, but armored in calm, and the alert brown one, her full lips parted, points of yellow light dancing in her eyes as she laughed and chattered. (p. 135)

Rural subjects set in heroic poses and rendered in a pastoral mood—these qualities link *O Pioneers!* with the art of Breton. But in Cather's appeal to the creative imagination, *O Pioneers!* is closer to Millet's art than to that of Breton. Breton tended to send a message to a relatively passive observer; his carefully selected and rendered details, his human figures positioned in symbolic poses, even his titles, which summarize the central idea of the painting—all combine to do so. In this telling and its accompanying deemphasis on creativity and imagination, Breton was unlike Millet and the later Impressionists, for whom the artist's individualism was "the very guarantee of his creativity. Nature, in their eyes, [was] a neutral set of forms until animated by the artist's feelings."[12]

In the manner of Millet and the Impressionists, Cather evokes a creative, imaginative response in *O Pioneers!*. The novel tells of the transformation of the land, presenting Nebraska as a flat, empty country that slumbers until Alexandra awakens it by perceiving in it order and beauty. Like the Impressionists, Cather uses light and color for that transforming perception, to deemphasize objects, and to present the mind in the act of perceiving. Women shopping are flashes of red and plaid (p. 4), fields are a medley of "green and brown and yellow" (p. 75), and Alexandra is "white and gold" (p. 135). "When the sun was hanging low over the wheatfield," trees were dark shades in light, a scene Cather interprets by principles of Impressionism: "Long fingers of light reached through the apple branches as through a net; the orchard was riddled and shot with gold; light was the reality, the trees were merely interferences that reflected and refracted light" (p. 258).

A peasant subject treated in the pastoral mode and with images that appeal to the reader's creative imagination, it is a combination that works well in *O Pioneers!*, but one that Cather did not repeat in her next novel. For *The Song of the Lark* (1915), Cather moved away from the manner of Millet and aligned herself more closely with that of Breton. She did so with her full, detailed narrative, and she did so with specific allusions to Breton, using the title of his painting for her title, describing that painting as the catalyst of a major awakening scene, and allowing the painted scene to appear in simplified form on the original dust jacket of her novel [fig. 37].

As in *O Pioneers!*, Cather employed native materials for her setting and characters. *The Song of the Lark* tells of Thea Kronborg's growing up in the small town of Moonstone, Colorado (based on Red Cloud, Nebraska). Thea is in some ways similar to Cather's other immigrant characters, a girl with the strength, independence, and physique of an Old World peasant. But she is essentially different from them, for an artistic soul is hidden in her peasant's body. She releases this "second self" by moving from Moonstone into the larger world, where she discovers art first in Chicago and later in New York. For the artistic growth requisite to her, she must overcome her own provincialism. When she comes to Chicago she wears comically inappropriate costumes: she sings in a "Moonstone party dress," white organdy with a blue

sash, with which she wears "high heavy shoes which needed blacking."[13] Her ignorance about social conventions signals an artistic nature that is similarly ignorant. She seems heavy, slow—even stupid at times; she describes herself as "like a fat horse turning a sorghum mill" (p. 177), and she sometimes seems impervious to suggestion, "as if she were deaf" (p. 191). For Thea, primitivism is not a pastoral convention but a reality that carries with it painful imprisonment. Responding to art she is unable to understand, Thea seems like someone reared as a savage, then brought into a culture for which she is totally unprepared. When Thea heard music, she "retreated to a corner and became sullen or troubled" and "her face was the picture of restless misery. She would sit crouching forward, her elbows on her knees, her brows drawn together and her grey-green eyes smaller than ever, reduced to mere pinpoints of cold, piercing light" (p. 178).

Fig. 37. Illustration on dust jacket of Cather's *The Song of the Lark*, 1915. For assistance in obtaining a copy of the dust jacket, the author is grateful to Joan Crane, Curator of American Literature Collections, Rare Book Department, Alderman Library, University of Virginia.

It is for this character that Cather uses Breton's *The Song of the Lark.* Thea is one of those raw Midwesterners who "have seen their first and only good pictures" in the Chicago Art Institute.[14] Her response is unsophisticated but genuine:

> There was a picture—oh, that was the thing she ran up stairs so fast to see! That was her picture. She imagined that nobody cared for it but herself, and that it waited for her. That was a picture indeed. She liked even the name of it, "The Song of the Lark." The flat country, the early morning light, the wet fields, the look in the girl's heavy face—well, they were all hers, anyhow, whatever was there. She told herself that that picture was "right." Just what she meant by this, it would take a clever person to explain. But to her the word covered the almost boundless satisfaction she felt when she looked at the picture. (p. 197)

In *O Pioneers!* Cather had described Alexandra's awakening as if a scene from one of Breton's paintings; for Thea's awakening she included the painting itself. Both scenes involve a character's possession of her own region, a transformation of a previously alien world into one that is personal. Alexandra's eyes drink in the breadth of the land and absorb it, until the history of the country begins in her heart; Thea recognizes that "the flat country, the early morning light, the wet fields, the look in the girl's heavy face—well, they were all hers." Finally, both rely upon the ordering hand of art to filter reality through a pastoral tradition by which the real is suppressed in favor of an ideal.

Yet in Cather's writing this suppression is never complete, perhaps because so much in her own experience contradicted that attitude. Though she appreciated the beauty of her native Nebraska, she was too aware of its harshness to rhapsodize over nature as a Garden of Eden, as Breton did in his memoirs, *La Vie d'un Artiste.*[15] And while she valued the security of a small town, like Thea Kronborg she railed against the provincialism of its people. Her early essays and stories contain bleak accounts of bitter struggle against hostile nature and small-minded communities, a struggle that appears in *O Pioneers!* as an undercurrent to the dominant sunny mood. After the initial creative pioneering work is completed, Alexandra recognizes the limitations of the society she has helped to form: "we grow hard and heavy here. . .and our minds get stiff. If the world were no wider than my cornfields, if there were not something beside [*sic*] this, I wouldn't feel that it was much worth while to work" (p. 124). Nowhere is Alexandra's sense of restriction better illustrated than in the self-satisfied provincialism of her brothers and their families, characterizations that are among the most harshly satiric in Cather's fiction.

An undercurrent in the later sections of *O Pioneers!*, struggle against rural provincialism is a major theme in *The Song of the Lark,* in which Cather "set out to tell of an artist's awakening and struggle; her floundering escape from a smug, domestic, self-satisfied world of utter ignorance."[16] Thea Kronborg does not come to terms with her region so much as leave it; she feels "boundless satisfaction" not from any firsthand experience of her native materials but about a painting that, by ordering and composing them, has made them "right." There is a certain irony in Cather's use of Breton's painting. While Breton painted a peasant girl awakening to the rural beauty about her, Cather wrote of a peasant girl awakening to the beauty of an art that enables her to escape from her own neighborhood. Moreover, the story of Thea's escape from her region weakens as she does so. As Cather recognized, the further *The Song of the Lark* went from her character's personal life (and by implication the more she left her rural materials), the paler the story became.

Cather eventually believed she had taken a wrong turn with *The Song of the Lark.* In her 1932 preface to the revised edition, she wrote that she regretted the "full blooded method" she had used, a detailed narrative that tended to tell the reader rather than to work by suggestion. She regretted also her use of Breton's painting for her title, for many readers "take it for granted that the 'lark song' refers to the vocal accomplishments of the heroine, which is altogether a mistake. Her song was not the skylark order." Cather intended the picture and its title to refer to Thea's awakening to something beautiful, not to the bird's song.[17] By dissociating the experience of beauty from an experience of nature, Cather suggests conflict that remained unresolved in her own responses to her native materials. She recognized their importance to her art, yet the realities of rural life included elements antithetical to the pastoral manner she had used to treat them.

It is a tension Cather incorporated into the narrative strategy of her next novel, *My Ántonia,* by counterpointing the two strains of the rural tradition represented by Breton and Millet. She used as her narrator Jim Burden, who has left Nebraska and is recalling the past from a distance made safe by economic and class privilege as well as by time. In his recollection of the Nebraska of his childhood as a time and place of idyllic pleasures, Burden reveals an attitude similar to that of Jules Breton's paintings. Breton, as Hollister Sturges writes, painted in the tradition of a

> benign vision of peasant culture and rural manners. . .that dates back to an agrarian creed found in classical antiquity

Fig. 38. Jean-François Millet, *The Sower,* oil on canvas, 40 × 32½ in. Museum of Fine Arts, Boston, Gift of Quincy Adams Shaw through Quincy A. Shaw Jr. and Mrs. Marian Shaw Haughton.

and expressed in Virgil's *Georgics*. . . . [T]he pastoral was the conception of the courtier or cosmopolite and was his means of gaining access to a nature of eternal spring and bountiful harvests—a benevolent nature in which the struggles of tilling the soil were reduced to cupid's play. . . . By concealing hardship, peasant crudeness and discontent, such art charms and delights but avoids difficult social questions and unseemly contact with reality.[18]

The description could be of Jim Burden, who recalls and implicitly identifies with Virgil's words on the *Georgics:* "For I shall be the first, if I live, to bring the Muse into my country . . . not a nation or even a province, but [my] own little 'country'; . . . [my] father's fields." (p. 264)

Jim wishes to fit Ántonia into this pastoral world. He would make her into an Alexandra, coming out of the morning carrying her milk pails. To do so, he denies all that would spoil his idyll, angrily turning away from her when she is coarsened by field work; feeling disgust when she has an affair and, unwed, bears a child; and

years later, dreading meeting her for fear she will have aged and, by doing so, will destroy his "illusions" of her.[19]

At the same time Cather presents Jim Burden in the manner of Breton, she presents Ántonia and the other immigrants in the manner of Millet [fig. 38]. They have a strength and monumental reality that contradict Jim's attempts to soften them. Ántonia *is* bent over the fields and she *is* coarsened by the back-breaking labor of planting and plowing. The effects of her labor are inescapable: in the perspiration that gathers on her upper lip, in the men's clothing that covers her body, in her sun-burned arms and throat, and in her strong, muscular neck. Her actions further present the reality of her labor. Following a day in the fields, she kept "lifting and dropping her shoulders as if they were stiff" (p. 123), and at supper she "ate noisily. . . like a man, and she yawned often at the table and kept stretching her arms over her

Fig. 39. Jean-François Millet, *The Gleaners,* 1857, oil on canvas, 32⅞ × 43¾ in. Musée du Louvre, Paris.

head, as if they ached" (p. 125). Such actions present the physical realities that Jim Burden seeks to deny as surely as the sculptural weight of the women in Millet's *The Gleaners* [fig. 39] suggests the labor that, as Cather said, has made them "warped and bowed and heavy."[20]

Just as Ántonia is coarsened by work, she is aged by time. When Jim returns to Nebraska after twenty years, he finds not an Alexandra who "has become sunnier, more vigorous with passing time," but an Ántonia who has become "a stalwart, brown woman, flat-chested, her curly brown hair a little grizzled" (p. 331). She speaks to Jim through a mouth in which teeth are missing, and she extends to him her calloused "hard-worked hands." Jim's initial reaction is shock, but gradually he recognizes Ántonia's strength and identity. Significantly, Cather does not deny the individual in bringing art to her native land, as she did in *O Pioneers!*. Indeed, Ántonia becomes more real, more human as the book continues, and it is by the force of her reality and individuality that Jim comes to recognize that she is a symbol, "a rich mine of races" (p. 353).

My Ántonia concludes with tension between two impulses—one pastoral and the other realistic. Though she had given Ántonia the strength to resist Jim's desire to transform her into a pastoral shepherdess, Cather does not deny this pastoral vision, but affirms its value as a release from dehumanizing pressures of a modern world. In the end, Jim has found a golden world reminiscent of Breton, where he can sleep in the straw, watch "haystacks turn rosy in the slanting sunlight" (p. 371), and play with children. Yet it is a pastoral world that has been given vigor of historical reality by an Ántonia who, in the manner of Millet, has weight and substance, who coarsens and ages. In this conclusion *My Ántonia* does not resolve differences, nor does it celebrate a communal vision. Instead, it affirms possibilities of a dramatic tension between a utopian ideal and a historical reality. Cather's genius lies in bringing together these two impulses of her European models not in resolution, but in ongoing, creative opposition. In so doing, she brought the Muse to her own region.

Notes

1. Robert Herbert, *Jean-François Millet* (London: Arts Council of Great Britain, 1976), p. 10.

2. Willa Cather, "My First Novels [There Were Two]," in *Willa Cather on Writing* (New York: Alfred A. Knopf, 1949), pp. 94-95.

3. Edith Lewis, *Willa Cather Living: A Personal Record* (New York: Alfred A. Knopf, 1953), p. 17.

4. I am using the basic definition of genre art as "a type of picture. . .depicting. . .everyday life and surroundings. . . . The important thing is that it should not represent idealized life." Peter Murray

and Linda Murray, *A Dictionary of Art and Artists*, 3rd ed. (Baltimore: Penguin Books, 1972). Cather's interest in Dutch genre painting is evident in her later writing also, especially in *The Professor's House*. See Cather's comment on Dutch painting in "On the Professor's House," in *Willa Cather on Writing*, pp. 31-32, and Patricia Yongue's essay, "Willa Cather's *The Professor's House* and Dutch Genre Painting," *Renascence* 31 (Spring 1979):155-67.

5. In *Willa Cather's Collected Short Fiction, 1892-1912*, ed. Virginia Faulkner with an introduction by Mildred R. Bennett (Lincoln: University of Nebraska Press, 1965), pp. 28-29.

6. James Woodress, *Willa Cather: Her Life and Art* (1970; Bison Book ed., Lincoln: University of Nebraska Press, 1975), pp. 102-03.

7. See, for example, Cather's reference to Millet in an interview, 9 August 1913, for the *Special Correspondence* of the [Philadelphia] Record, in *The Kingdom of Art: Willa Cather's First Principles and Critical Statements, 1893-1896*, selected and edited with a commentary by Bernice Slote (Lincoln: University of Nebraska Press, 1966), p. 447; and a similar reference to Millet in her 1920 essay, "On the Art of Fiction," in *Willa Cather on Writing*.

8. From the *Courier*, 10 August 1901, p. 2, in *The World and the Parish: Willa Cather's Articles and Reviews 1893-1902*, selected and edited with a commentary by William M. Curtin, 2:842-46.

9. Ibid., pp. 842-43.

10. From flyleaf dedication of Carrie Miner Sherwood's copy of *O Pioneers!*, quoted by Mildred R. Bennett, *The World of Willa Cather*, rev. ed. with notes and index (Bison Book ed., Lincoln: University of Nebraska Press, 1961), illus., n.p.

11. Cather, *O Pioneers!* (1913; Sentry ed., Boston: Houghton Mifflin, 1962), p. 65. Hereafter quotations from *O Pioneers!* will be from this edition and included in the text. For a more complete discussion of *O Pioneers!* as pastoral, see Susan J. Rosowski, *The Voyage Perilous: Willa Cather's Romanticism* (Lincoln: University of Nebraska Press, 1986), pp. 45-61.

12. Herbert, p. 13.

13. Cather, *The Song of the Lark* (1915; Bison Book ed., Lincoln: University of Nebraska Press, 1978), pp. 179-80. Hereafter quotations from *The Song of the Lark* will be from this edition and included in the text. The 1915 edition is more detailed in manner and more strident in tone than the revised version.

14. *The World and the Parish*, p. 843.

15. Jules Breton, *La Vie d'un Artiste: Art et Nature* (Paris, 1890), trans. Mary J. Serrano, *The Life of an Artist: An Autobiography* (New York: D. Appleton and Company, 1890).

16. "Preface" written in 1932 for the revised *Song of the Lark* (Boston: Houghton Mifflin Company, 1937), p. v.

17. Ibid., pp. v-vi.

18. Hollister Sturges, "Jules Breton and the French Rural Tradition," in *Jules Breton and the French Rural Tradition*, exhibition catalogue, (Omaha, Neb.: Joslyn Art Museum, 1982), p. 10. For a discussion of Cather's place in the epic tradition, see Paul A. Olson, "The Epic and Great Plains Literature: Rølvaag, Cather, and Neihardt," *Prairie Schooner* 55 (Spring/Summer 1981):263-85. Professor Olson argues that Plains literature in the epic mode "succeeds because the plains writers created nonformulaic methods of presentation appropriate to the heroism of peasant peoples, of women, and of minority groups" (p. 265), and that "Cather invents in *My Ántonia* a 'georgic epic' " (p. 278).

19. Cather, *My Ántonia* (1918; Sentry ed., Boston: Houghton Mifflin Company, 1961), p. 328. Hereafter quotations from *My Ántonia* will be from this edition and included in the text.

20. When visiting at Barbizon, Cather wrote of "the gleaners—usually women who looked old and battered, who were bent and slow and not much good for much else. . . . As the sun dropped lower the merriment ceased; the women were tired and grew to look more and more as Millet painted them, warped and bowed and heavy." 21 September 1902, in *The World and the Parish*, p. 931.

Detail Fig. 55. Eastman Johnson, *Cornhusking Bee.*

Images of Rural America in the Works of
Eastman Johnson, Winslow Homer, and Their Contemporaries
A Survey and Critique

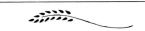

© *by Patricia Hills*

PAINTERS. Their works are at once their actions and their history,
and a record of the taste and feelings of the times in which they flourished.
—*A. Cunningham,* The Crayon *(February 1859)*

ESTABLISHED American painters of rural life who exhibited in the major annuals from 1830 to 1880 showed little interest in actual farming as it was being industrialized and modernized in that fifty-year period. Instead, their most popular and critically acclaimed subjects of farm life portrayed a preindustrial era, when farm production was small-scale, communal, and labor-intensive.[1] This phenomenon, this seeming anachronism, does not mean our painters were ignorant about agri-business, about the fact that at mid century reaper-mowers, mechanical threshers, and other farm machinery were transforming farms from subsistence operations into commercial enterprises.[2] Indeed, our artists felt no inclination to introduce modernized farm implements and equipment as motifs in their paintings because the documentation of modern farm life was not on their agenda.

What our artists deliberately painted were images aimed to please prospective patrons. If they chose scenes from traditional rural subject matter, it was because their patrons cherished such memories of a preindustrial era. An astute critic, writing in 1859, affirmed (with perhaps some irony) that:

> Exhibitions do not display the merits of particular works of Art and the progress of individual artists so much as they do the nature of public taste, or rather the character of artistic thought which the public chooses to manifest through its encouragement of Art. . . . It is a mistake to suppose that artists are free to paint what pleases them best. . . . The Truth is, that artists are compelled to meet the public by consulting its likes and dislikes.[3]

The public to which the critic refers was a cosmopolitan, entrepreneurial class that included, but certainly was not limited to, ambitious artists, critics, art dealers, and picture buyers. This last group, the patrons who could afford to buy pictures, shaped the course of American art. The old adage "he who pays the piper, calls the tune" was as true then as now.

At that time "artistic thought," referred to by the critic, was inseparable from "right sentiment." And painters knew that the subject alone did not sell pictures but, rather, the "sentiment"—the feelings of comfort induced in a patron when a picture matched his fond memories or pseudo-memories. But what our painters may not have been conscious of was the extent to which entrepreneurial values permeated the sentiment of the subject matter. These values, united with strong yearnings for a lost and more innocent youth, became the implicit, if not the explicit, content for a self-consciously "American" art.

Asher B. Durand, whose mid-century "Letters on Landscape Painting" for *The Crayon* influenced a generation of artists, was obviously aware of the desires paintings could evoke in a typical patron. His fourth "Letter" of 1855 deserves to be quoted at length because of its admission of the function of art: to soothe the nerves of the tired businessman.

> To the rich merchant and capitalist, and to those whom even a competency has released from the great world-struggle, so far as to allow a little time to rest and reflect in, Landscape Art especially appeals. . . .
> It becomes companionable, holding silent converse with the feelings, playful or pensive—and, at times, touching a chord that vibrates to the inmost recesses of the heart, yet with no unhealthy excitement, but soothing and strength-

ening to his best faculties. Suppose such an one, on his return home, after the completion of his daily task of drudgery—his dinner partaken, and himself disposed of in his favorite arm-chair, with one or more faithful landscapes before him, and making no greater effort than to look into the picture. . . so as to perceive what it represents; in proportion as it is true and faithful, many a fair vision of forgotten days will animate the canvas, and lead him through the scene: pleasant reminiscences and grateful emotions will spring up at every step, and care and anxiety will retire far behind him. . . . [He] becomes absorbed in the picture. . . . He shifts the scene, and stretching fields and green meadows meet his eye—in such he followed the plough and tossed the new-mown hay; by the road-side stands the school-house, and merry children scatter from its door—such was the place where he first imbibed the knowledge that the world was large and round, while ambition whispered that the village grounds were too narrow for him,—and with the last rays of the setting sun, the picture fades away.[4]

The significance of Durand's statement lies less in its prescription for favored and appealing subject matter than in its revelation of the values of the political economy of the Age of Laissez Nous Faire: capitalists achieve their goals through hard work (ploughing, tossing hay and, later, the drudgery of the office), education (the schoolhouse), and ambition.[5] In other words, Durand's statement and the paintings discussed here witness, to varying degrees, a set of values dearly held by the entrepreneurial middle classes of America. And those values were thought to be forged in the rural setting of the farm.

For the sake of our survey here, these values can be loosely grouped into two categories: first, that of individualism nurtured by participatory democracy. And second, that of entrepreneurial work—not just physical labor, but skills in mastering tools and, especially, cleverness in competing with others. These values came to define the essence of "Americanness." After all, Americans were not peasants. Their vote assured their status as free people inferior to no one, particularly Europeans with their aristocratic airs. And Americans welcomed work and extolled thrift, for all around them they could see men who had ascended into the upper ranks of society through work and cleverness.[6]

By asserting that the content of fine arts painting reflected "democratic" values, we should not gloss over the class nature of American society. Recent studies point not only to how stratified Americans in fact were, but also to their *awareness* of the inequities attached to class, race, and gender distinctions.[7] Without dwelling on statistics, we know (and they knew) that blacks and many propertyless white men were excluded from middle-class life. Moreover, the white women who shared the economic status of their fathers or husbands did not share their males' educational, intellectual, or political advantages, and they knew it. Nevertheless, compared to Europe the United States appeared classless, because we had no aristocracy in the European sense. Most of us chose to ignore the institution of slavery, and "we" were generically male. Democracy, though flawed, was viewed as an *American* institution.

So, too, entrepreneurial values were considered particularly *American*. The often quoted passage from Hector St. John de Crèvecoeur's *Letters from an American Farmer,* published in 1782, merits quotation at length for this affirmation of America as a nation of democratic yeomen.

[We] are all tillers of the earth, from Nova Scotia to West Florida. We are a people of cultivators, scattered over an immense territory, communicating with each other by means of good roads and navigable rivers, united by the silken bands of mild government, all respecting the laws without dreading their power, because they are equitable. We are all animated with the spirit of an industry which is unfettered and unrestrained, because each person works for himself. . . . Lawyer or merchant are the fairest titles our town afford; that of a farmer is the only appellation of the rural inhabitants of our country. . . . We have no princes for whom we toil, starve, and bleed; we are the most perfect society now existing in the world.[8]

Even though the farmer's lot was difficult (and agricultural and economic historians have calculated the hardships and deprivations of farm life to the average New York and New England farmer, particularly as America was being transformed into an industrialized society), the farmer became the hero of *the* myth of America, as Henry Nash Smith has argued.[9] A review of the most popular and typical genre paintings from the 1830 to 1880 period would confirm Smith's theory. Indeed, in the pictorial arts the images of the farmer and of rural life became primary vehicles for the transmission of the values of American individualism and entrepreneurialism.[10]

The paintings were, in fact, charged to do so. Many nineteenth-century American writers explicitly promoted the nationalist mission of genre painting. A writer for the *Cosmopolitan Art Journal* in June 1857 wrote:

Akin with every other utilitarian science, painting has its instructive mission, ever varying as the characteristics of the people change from progress of civilization. To be merely decorative, art fails of its object in invention; for it possesses a nobler purpose, which may be justly defined as the conservation of patriotism. As language keeps alive the fire of nationality, so should painting embalm the genius of a country by preserving memory of familiar scenes, or by transmitting to posterity reminiscences of actions, deeds, or manners.

The hour has arrived when the necessities of our country not only justify, but inexorably demand, the production of a series of national paintings.[11]

Especially at a time when the nation teetered on the verge of civil conflict, American painters compliantly and enthusiastically provided a series of optimistic, national paintings.[12]

What is offered here is a survey of images that transmit the values of the entrepreneurial classes through traditional, familiar, and seemingly anachronistic thematic situations and artistic motifs. And these values, presented simply or in combination, can be traced through a series of paintings beginning with John Lewis

Krimmel and culminating in Eastman Johnson, with Winslow Homer serving as the transition into a more modern era.[13]

The individualism nurtured by participatory democracy finds its most common pictorial visualization in the motif of newspapers. To have a voice in politics meant reading newspapers. Contemporary accounts frequently comment on Americans' voracious appetite for the news. In 1782 a writer for the *Virginia Gazette and American Advertiser,* complaining about the situation in Virginia and contrasting it with the North, asserted: "In the Eastern States the *People* are informed. The Gazettes circulate freely; the laws are promulgated before they are in force; the *People* know their situation, and keep a watchful eye over their servants."[14] And the Duke de la Rochefoucault-Liancourt in his *Travels Through the United States of North America,* published in 1799, observed of Massachusetts: "Not a house is to be found

Fig. 40. John Lewis Krimmel, *Village Tavern, Arrival of the Post with News of Peace,* 1813-14, oil on canvas, 16⅞ × 22½ in. The Toledo Museum of Art, Gift of Florence Scott Libbey.

Fig. 41. William Sidney Mount, *The* Herald *in the Country,* oil on panel, 17 × 13 in. The Museums at Stony Brook, New York, Gift of Mr. and Mrs. Ward Melville, 1953.

in the most remote corners of the country, where a newspaper is not read; and there are few townships which do not possess little libraries formed and supported by subscription."[15] The theme of reading newspapers appeared, I believe, in mid-nineteenth-century American genre painting with far greater frequency than in European painting.[16]

John Lewis Krimmel was a German painter who emigrated to Philadelphia in 1810 when he was twenty-one years old. Critics admired his adaptation of the style of the popular English painter David Wilkie to the subject matter of his new home. In the *Analectic Magazine* of February 1820, a reviewer advanced the opinion:

> [Krimmel] has painted many pictures in which the style of Wilkie—so much admired in England—and Gerard Dow so much celebrated of yore—is most successfully followed. He avoids the broad humor of the Flemish school as much as possible, as not congenial to the refinement of modern taste, and aims rather at a true portraiture of nature in real, rustic life.[17]

Krimmel's painting *Village Tavern, Arrival of the Post with News of Peace* of about 1814 [fig. 40] was one such picture that would have been considered "true," "real,"

"modern," and "native." It not only avoided coarseness and vulgarity by representing the village people with all their necessary dignity, but may well be the first American painting touching on this theme of participatory democracy—the everyday person's concern for the political future of the country. All the figures respond to the news, both oral and written. While most of the figures in the room listen to the messenger who has burst into the tavern, the old man at the right and the young boy by the stove at the left hold newspapers. Four more newspapers hang from rods hooked to the wall. Newspapers, as we shall see, did double duty in American painting by underscoring the value of mass education and by alluding to contemporary and topical events. Thirty years later the same subject had the same meaning: in James Goodwyn Clonney's *Mexican News* (1847, Munson-Williams-Proctor Institute, Utica, New York) and Richard Caton Woodville's *War News from Mexico* (1848, National Academy of Design, New York), the motif means that ordinary Americans are literate, keep abreast of the news, and perhaps even make the news. Woodville's image had a wide circulation; in 1851 it was engraved by the American Art-Union and distributed to

Fig. 42. Eastman Johnson, *The Evening Newspaper,* 1863, oil on academy board, 17 × 14 ½ in. Amherst College, Meade Art Museum, Gift of Herbert W. Plimpton, The Hollis W. Plimpton Memorial Collection.

its membership, which then numbered 13,578 subscribers throughout the country.[18]

Mount's painting *The* Herald *in the Country* (1853) [fig. 41] was first called *The Politics of 1852, or Who Let Down the Bars?* According to a contemporary description, a city person on a gunning trip lets down the fence bars in order to trespass onto a farmer's property. When the farmer appears, the hunter, in order to disarm his possible anger, engages him in a political discussion. Mount wrote in his journal for the year 1853: "Politics of 1852, or who let down the bars. Sold to Goupil Co. To be engraved in Paris. 'The Sturdy old farmer looks as if he was asking—'Come tell us what the news is, Who wins now, and who loses?" ' "[19] The historian could not hope for better affirmation of the political content of the newspaper motif.

In the early 1860s, the period of the Civil War, the newspaper motif could well refer to the farmer's concern for events in the war. The farmer in Eastman Johnson's *The Evening Newspaper* (1863) [fig. 42] has time for the latest news, maybe about farm prices but perhaps about the latest military campaigns as well. Relevant to our thesis, he looks at us as an equal, as if inviting a con-

versation. The solidity of his form and the poise of his expression counter-balance the precariousness of the tilt of his chair, and, by extension, the period in which he lives.

Democracy in action, rural men taking an active role in the political business of debating, campaigning for office, and voting, emerged as popular themes of many mid-century American paintings. To us, a number of them could serve as reminders of Alexis de Tocqueville's observations noted in *Democracy in America,* first published in 1835 and 1840, that:

> The people are . . . the real directing power; and although the form of government is representative, it is evident that the opinions, the prejudices, the interests, and even the passions of the people are hindered by no permanent obstacles from exercising a perpetual influence on the daily conduct of affairs.[20]

Paintings are, however, not *illustrations*—things that function as secondary to a text; rather, pictures are primary material that stand on their own, that came into being in a context similar to de Tocqueville's book, and were influential communicators of ideas in their own right. Yet, pictures and texts can corroborate or critique one another. While we may question the validity of the views behind de Tocqueville's words—whether they reflected actual circumstances or were merely a foreign observer's contribution to the developing mythology of America—we know he did not have in mind women and blacks. In the genre paintings of "the daily conduct of affairs," these two groups take their place at the periphery of the canvas, where they are mere onlookers to the boisterous scenes of white men arguing politics or a point of law. Such paintings with "peripheral" blacks and women at the edges or in the background include Clonney's *Politicians in a Country Bar* (1844, New York State Historical Association, Cooperstown), Woodville's *War News from Mexico,* and William Sydney Mount's *News from California* (1850, The Suffolk Museum and Carriage House, Stony Brook, New York).[21]

George Caleb Bingham specialized in such political scenes to a greater degree than any other genre painter.

He himself ran for political office in 1846 and 1848, losing the first time by a handful of votes, but winning a decisive election two years later. Art historian Robert Westervelt has asked us to look again at *The County Election* (1851-52) [fig. 43], a painting long considered a celebration of American politics.[22] Westervelt's thesis contends that Bingham, a disgruntled Whig, deplored the extension of the suffrage to the propertyless classes and satirized that issue in this particular painting. Here we see no women and only one black man, typically at the edge of the canvas. The many white men who crowd the scene are drinking, gesticulating, and arguing. Some are in a severe state of inebriation, even needing assistance up the stairs of the courthouse to vote. One politician on the steps makes a last-minute appeal to his constituency. On the porch column is tacked the notice: "The Will of the People the Supreme Law." Although Westervelt persuasively argues his point, I believe few Americans who saw the popular print wanted to see the

Fig. 43. George Caleb Bingham, *The County Election,* 1851-52, oil. The Boatman's National Bank of St. Louis.

work as an indictment of the political system. The "low-class" characters were probably good-naturedly acknowledged by the art audience as standard types present on election days.[23]

More optimistic images of male suffrage occurred during the immediate post-Civil War period, when Northern expectations ran high regarding the fortunes of the recently freed slaves. A case in point—and such pictures are rare—is Thomas Waterman Wood's *His First Vote,* painted about 1868 [fig. 44]. The black man's face expresses hope as he walks to the polls with his ballot in hand. Wood's optimism would have been short-lived, since the realities of Reconstruction soon shattered the dream of political equality. Such images of blacks as citizens integrated into white society do not survive past the late 1860s.[24] In the 1870s Wood returned to more successful formula for genre painting with the portrayal of two elderly men arguing in a barn in *The Day Before the Election* of 1875 (T. W. Wood Art Gallery, Montpelier, Vermont).

The leaders of mid-century genre painting—William Sidney Mount, George Caleb Bingham, and later Eastman Johnson and Winslow Homer—consistently showed the dignity of rural work while celebrating the shrewdness of the Yankee farmer. Such paintings were considered modern. The successful wholesale grocer and art patron Lumen Reed wrote to Mount on November 23, 1835, describing his pleasure in owning Mount's *Bargaining for a Horse* (1835) [fig. 45].

> This is a new era in the fine arts in this Country, we have native talent and it is coming out as rapidly as is necessary. Your picture of the "Bargain" is the wonder and delight of everyone that sees it.[25]

This "new era," "native" painting was reproduced as an engraving by the American Art-Union and distributed in 1851 along with Woodville's *War News from Mexico.* Thus, through the medium of prints, an image of forthright entrepreneurialism—"driving a bargain"—had a nationwide circulation and achieved considerable popularity.

Reed's remarks could have applied as well to Mount's *Farmer Whetting His Scythe* (1848) [fig. 46], exhibited the following year at the National Academy of Design and subsequently sold to the American Art-Union. The theme of work skills is made explicit as the farmer cares for his tools and the quality of his workmanship. Although mechanization was revolutionizing farm labor at the very same time, Mount chose not to show that kind of progress.

Fig. 44. Thomas Waterman Wood, *His First Vote,* c. 1868, oil on canvas, 20 × 11 in. Courtesy the Cincinnati (Ohio) Art Galleries.

Frank Blackwell Mayer's *Leisure and Labor* (1858) [fig. 47] contrasts virtuous work with indolent idleness. We look with some disdain on the rich young man leaning lazily against the door frame as the village blacksmith shoes the horse. The young man's clothes and his elegant greyhound disclose his wealth. The sign on the door, "Stop Theif [sic]," represents Father Time racing along. The message is clear: time robs us of our youth. With time running out, far better to fill the day with work than with indolence.[26]

Since maintaining the values of individualism and entrepreneurialism—and our sense of Americanness—

Fig. 45. William Sidney Mount, *Bargaining for a Horse.* The New-York Historical Society, New York City.

Fig. 46. William Sidney Mount, *Farmer Whetting His Scythe,* 1848, oil on canvas, 24 × 20 in. The Museums at Stony Brook, New York, Gift of Mr. and Mrs. Ward Melville, 1955.

Fig. 47. Frank Blackwell Mayer, *Leisure and Labor,* oil on canvas. The Corcoran Gallery of Art, Gift of William Wilson Corcoran.

Fig. 48. Charles Caleb Ward, *Force and Skill,* oil on canvas. The Currier Gallery of Art, Manchester, New Hampshire.

meant reminding ourselves of the importance of preparing children, through education and with exemplary role models, to assume their future responsibilities, it is not surprising that many popular genre paintings depicted children in farm settings, acting out the roles of adults. The thematic message assured the viewer of the stability to society when children prepare for their future tasks and responsibilities. Charles Caleb Ward's painting *Force and Skill* (1869) [fig. 48] underscores the moral that both brawn and brains are needed to do a job properly; that is, no division occurs between manual and mental labor. This message came at a time when industrialization had increased the division between the two. The parent ducks and their ducklings in the lower right corner reinforce the multiple morals: the young boys' cooperative work will lead to happy, productive adult lives. Art patrons would not have found pleasure in pictures of strife and conflict. In many of Eastman Johnson's paintings and those of J. G. Brown, such as *The Industrious Family* (private collection), younger children are shown learning from their elders.[27]

The cumulative message adds up to this: the farmer is heroic, virtuous, bargains well, reads the newspaper, and is made of the stuff of the "true American."[28] Politicians certainly drew on this image in their rhetoric. Representative George W. Julian of Indiana, in an 1851 speech in favor of offering free land to settlers, said:

> The life of a farmer is peculiarly favorable to virtue; and both individuals and communities are generally happy in proportion as they are virtuous. His manners are simple, and his nature unsophisticated. If not oppressed by other interests, he generally possesses an abundance without the drawback of luxury. His life does not impose excessive toil, and yet it discourages idleness. The farmer lives in rustic plenty, remote from the contagion of popular vices, and enjoys, in their greatest fruition, the blessings of health and contentment.[29]

Although Representative Julian voiced a common sentiment, one should beware of taking his statement at face value. He may very well have had some political and economic interests tied to the settlement of Indiana. There were certainly political and economic motivations behind the Homestead Act, passed in 1862, which allowed settlers 160 acres of land. The North, after all, wanted the homesteaders as a buffer against the slave-owning South. One-hundred-sixty acres of farmland could not support the system of slavery—a system, aside from its inhumanity, that was economically unprogressive compared to that of wage labor being developed by the Northern industrialists.[30] Whether conscious of the fact or not, painters who specialized in pictures of Yankee farmers were tapping into a pro-North market.

Eastman Johnson (1824-1906) and Winslow Homer (1836-1916) inherited the legacy of the genre tradition developing in America, but they were also innovators in terms of subject matter. Born in Maine, where his father was involved first with state and then with national politics, Johnson studied for almost six years in Düsseldorf, The Hague, and Paris. He returned to the United States in the mid 1850s and began to carve a solid reputation as a painter of American subjects. During the 1860s he was one of the few American genre painters who chose Civil War subjects.

Homer was born in Boston of solid middle-class parentage. His father was in the hardware business for a time, with a brief sojourn in California during the Gold Rush. Homer began working for Boston lithography firms in the 1850s and, with the commencement of the war, joined the Union troops at the front. His success with Civil War illustrations for *Harper's Weekly* encouraged him to try his hand at painting the same subjects. Without a doubt, during the 1860s Johnson was the most admired of the established genre painters, and Homer, the most promising. Both knew contemporary European painting, and each artist's work lends itself to transcontinental comparisons.[31]

Johnson's *Woodcutter* (c. 1862, Smith College Museum of Art) represents the model pioneer farmer, who stands erect and commanding. He has just felled large tree, presumably with little effort. In the iconography of nineteenth-century America, the cut tree symbolized progress: tree stumps meant that civilization was triumphing over the wilderness.[32] Johnson's farmer contrasts tellingly with the older rural proletarian in Gustave Courbet's famous painting, *The Stone Breakers* of 1851 (destroyed in 1945). The latter's facial features are in shadow; he is mindless brawn engaged in endless labor, his body and limbs a set of gears turning monotonously. There is no hint of relief—just endless repetitive work.

Johnson's *Winnowing Grain,* done in the early 1860s [fig. 49], makes a similar contrast with European painting. Johnson's farmer seems to work effortlessly—pouring a shower of gold which will eventually fill his own pockets. The anonymous peasant of Jean-François Millet's *The Winnower* of 1848 [fig. 50] is burdened by the heavy load of the landlord's grain.

Unlike Johnson, Winslow Homer received no European training, but his trip to France in 1866-67, in part to see the Paris Exposition, made considerable impact on

Fig. 49. Eastman Johnson, *Winnowing Grain,* 1873-79, oil on chipboard, 15½ × 13 in. Museum of Fine Arts, Boston, M. and M. Karolik Collection.

Fig. 50. Jean-François Millet, *The Winnower,* oil, 31¼ × 23, Musée du Louvre, Paris.

Fig. 51. Winslow Homer, *The Return of the Gleaner,* 1867, oil on canvas, 24 × 18 in. Margaret Woodbury Strong Museum, Rochester, New York.

his art. Although previously in America he had done paintings of farm workers in the fields, such as *Veteran in a New Field* (1865, The Metropolitan Museum of Art, New York) and *Haymaking* (1864, Columbus Museum of Art, Ohio), on a visit to Picardy he turned his eye to French peasant women. *Return of the Gleaner* (1867) [fig. 51] and *Girl with Pitchfork* (1867, The Phillips Collection, Washington, D.C.) were the results of this sojourn. However, these Homer women are not the comely beauties of such French artists as Jules Breton and William Bouguereau, nor are they the generalized, almost Biblical, personages of Millet. Rather, the expressions on the women's faces suggest solidity and fortitude—neither sentimental nor eroticized. Perhaps Homer's own view of American farmers influenced the forthrightness with which he portrayed the female French peasant.

Back in America in the 1870s, Homer continued the theme of farm workers, painting *A Gloucester Farm* in 1874 (Philadelphia Museum of Art) and *Milking Time* in 1875 (Delaware Art Museum, Wilmington). He also painted farm children in school or playing in fields adjacent to the schoolhouse. With Homer, American art began to move away from the moralizing genre of mid

century toward a naturalism minimizing anecdotal, moralizing, or patriotic content.

However, two final works in Homer's *oeuvre* beg comparison with European examples. *Answering the Horn* (1876) [fig. 52] was exhibited at the National Academy of Design in 1877, and *Song of the Lark* (1876) [fig. 53] at the Century Club in February 1877 and at the National Academy of Design the following year.[33] The two figures standing in a harvested field at twilight in *Answering the Horn* contrast with the couple in Millet's popular and widely reproduced painting, *The Angelus* (1857-59) [fig. 54]. Unlike the humble, pious French peasants, Homer's figures hold their heads high, alert to their environment. Similarly, we might compare Homer's farmer in *Song of the Lark,* who looks skyward as he pauses to listen to the bird, with the barefoot girl in Breton's *Song of the Lark* (1884) [fig. 36]. Homer's stalwart figure has his booted legs planted solidly on the ground, his hat and scythe held firmly, and his handsome face silhouetted against the grove of trees in the distant twilight. He is prepared for any shifts in the weather. He is no peasant, but a heroic individual who works for himself. Breton's figure, with her open, gap-

ing mouth, trods the earth barefoot, to inherit it only upon death.

What is obvious in our survey and, indeed, characterizes all pre-1880 American genre paintings of rustic life, is the overwhelming number of men as subjects: solid, suffrage-conscious male farmers. Perhaps the reasons rest on the fact that the themes needed to reinforce our positive attitudes about our country—the virtue of farm life and participatory democracy—were themes of, by, and for men. Women do appear, usually in harvest rather than planting scenes. Men plant the seeds; women help to produce the harvest. Although a sexual-psychological dimension to this gender preference may be operating, a simpler and naturalistic explanation is that planting does not require great numbers of people; the men in the family can handle the job. Whereas the amplitude of the harvest requires the participation of all.[34]

Johnson, indelibly stamped by mid-century notions of morality and nationalism, and twelve years older than Homer, did a well-known series on the harvesting of maple sugar in Maine in the early 1860s. Women participate in the festivities, as do the children and the old people. The sugaring-off celebration—at least as we see it in

the Johnson paintings—is a communal affair with everyone helping out. Knowing, as we do now, that this was a time when the ideals of communitarianism were disappearing along with the actuality of non-wage, cooperative farm work, these paintings seem nostalgic reminders of a passing age. But done when they were—very likely during the Civil War—they would have reminded Northerners of the traditions of their own region.

During the 1870s Johnson continued to paint pictures of community life on Nantucket, where he summered. One contemporary critic noted of Johnson and Nantucket: "The man and the place have a natural sympathy for each other. He is a chronicler of a phase of our national life which is fast passing away."[35] His *Cornhusking Bee* of 1876 [fig. 55] represents a panorama of farm people at work. A detail shows a young man who has husked a red ear, which entitles him, according to rural tradition, to kiss the woman next to him. At that time Johnson also undertook his most ambitious group of pictures to date—paintings of cranberry pickers. The series culminated in *The Cranberry Harvest* (1880) [fig. 56]. Several motifs in this work can be traced to popu-

Fig. 52. Winslow Homer, *Answering the Horn,* 1876, oil on canvas on board, 38⅛ × 24⅜ in. Muskegon (Michigan) Museum of Art.

Fig. 53. Winslow Homer, *Song of the Lark,* 1876, oil on canvas, 38⅝ × 24¼ in. The Chrysler Museum, Norfolk, Virginia, Gift of Walter P. Chrysler, Jr.

Fig. 54. Jean-François Millet, *The Angelus,* 1857-59, oil on canvas, 21⅞ × 26 in. Musée du Louvre, Paris.

lar European paintings. The standing woman in the middle of the canvas looking off to the right reminds us of the standing figure in Jules Breton's *The Weeders* (1860) [fig. 17], a painting known in America. The three figures bending over recall Millet's *The Gleaners* (1857) [fig. 39], another popular and widely reproduced French painting. Both French works have an elegiac mood; the Johnson painting, in contrast, is joyful and celebratory.

Rural themes in nineteenth-century art and literature provide us with a measure of the cultural protest against the negative manifestations of the industrial revolution—overcrowded city slums, urban pollution, and human exploitation. Millet, by all accounts, responded by venerating the poor and anonymous peasants as the last surviving species from a time in which human labor

had nobility and dignity. Breton, so we are told, understood the changing social and legal status of gleaners, resulting from the industrial revolution, and sympathized with their struggles for survival. Johnson, on the other hand, did not so much react against urban realities as ignore their very existence. No poor people inhabit Johnson's America; his figures are classless, rural Yankees working gaily and effortlessly, joking and flirting as they move from bog to bog in the autumn afternoon sun. His vision was praised by his earliest biographer, William Walton, who wrote in 1906:

He . . . preaches no ugly gospel of discontent, as does so much of the contemporary French and Flemish art of this genre; his Nantucket neighbors know nothing of the *protestation douloureuse de la race asservie à la glèbe;* there is

Fig. 55. Eastman Johnson, *Cornhusking Bee,* 1876, oil on canvas, 31½ × 50 in. The Art Institute of Chicago, the Potter Palmer Collection.

no *cri de la terre* arising from his cranberry marshes or his hay-stuffed barns.[36]

This is the point of American genre painting—that it "preaches no ugly gospel of discontent." When it does, we call it *realism,* not genre painting. In the vision of our country favored by Durand's "rich merchant and capitalist" disposed "in his favorite arm chair," pictorial images of old-fashioned life on the farm served as a necessary balm. Child labor, industrial accidents, and strikes had no place in such after-dinner relaxations.

In the late 1870s the majority of artists, particularly the younger painters, turned to the urban environment for pictorial themes. The subjects that emerged as most popular to the painters of modern life involved art and music, leisure-time and vacation activities, and urban sports.[37] A subtle shift in values began to emphasize consumerism and internationalism in place of entrepreneurialism and Americanism.

In summation: Given the fact that these farm images were anachronistic, why did the farmer and the preindustrial farm hold the attention of our art patrons for so long? The answer is simple. The pictures are about values, not about farming. The farm represented the best of the older *ideal of community,* and the farmer represented the best of the newer values of *entrepreneurial individualism.* In the period in transition from 1830 to 1880, from the ethos of cooperation to one of ruthless, and social Darwinian, competition, the *idea* of the farmer seemed to combine the best of both worlds. Not insignificantly, images of farm life also reminded us of the ongoing necessity of land settlement in the West in order to create a stronger, more self-reliant nation. And, finally, images of farm life denied the existence of an economically privileged class and made us forget the increasing conflicts between labor and the industrialists.

However, by the 1890s—the years of the Progressive movement that came out of the Midwest—Eastern patrons began to change their minds about farmers. They began to view farmers as a stubborn group making increasingly unreasonable demands on the nation's economy. In that decade Hamlin Garland wrote *Main-Traveled Roads,* a more realistic sketch of the rural scene, and none of the major painters—neither Johnson nor Homer—painted farm life. Johnson had turned to portraits, and Homer was doing his series of great sea pictures. Lesser artists, such as Thomas Waterman Wood and Edward Lamson Henry, still mined this now-exhausted vein, turning out pictures with a cloying, sentimental vapidity. The younger artists of talent, such as John Singer Sargent, Childe Hassam, and William Merritt Chase, had turned to holiday subjects and the cosmopolitan urban scene. Moreover, this younger group had overthrown the earlier moral imperative that paintings must teach lessons and had moved toward the creed of art-for-art's sake.[38]

But before the 1880s, before the realization came (covertly if not overtly) to the painters and their patrons that the farmer's viability as a cultural symbol was limited, Johnson rode high in popularity. His optimism and his celebration of the joys of rural labor—a labor in which the distinctions between working class and middle class were blurred—endeared him to a generation. Much of his appeal and his "Americanness," for them as well as for us, lies in his nostalgic vision of a preindustrial, essentially classless society involved in *American* tasks.

Notes

Author's Note: I first gave a lecture on the farmer in art at the Grolier Club, New York, in April 1975 entitled "The Farmer in American Art, 1830-1870: Country Bumpkin or the New Adam?" based on the section devoted to rural life in my *The Painters' America: Rural and Urban Life, 1810-1910* (New York: Praeger Publishers in Association with the Whitney Museum of American Art, 1974). Since 1982, after I delivered a substantially revised paper at the Joslyn Art Museum, important publications have appeared on the rural image in European painting. The present essay has been reworked in response to Richard R. Brettell and Caroline B. Brettell, *Painters and Peasants in the Nineteenth Century* (New York: Rizzoli International Publications, Inc., 1983); Gabriel P. Weisberg, ed., *The European Realist Tradition* (Bloomington: Indiana University Press, 1982); and, of course, Hollister Sturges, *Jules Breton and the French Rural Tradition* (Omaha, Neb.: Joslyn Art Museum, 1982). An important review of these three publications that calls for a sharpening of the theoretical issues is Griselda Pollock, "Revising or Reviving Realism?," *Art History* 7 (September 1984):359-68. I want also to call attention to Robert L. Herbert, "City vs. Country, the Rural Image in French Painting from Millet to Gauguin," *Artforum* 8 (February 1970):44-55; Gabriel P. Weisberg, *The Realist Tradition: French Paint-*

ing and Drawing, 1830-1900 (Cleveland: The Cleveland Museum of Art, 1980); and James Thompson, with the assistance of Madeleine Fidell Beaufort and John Horne, *The Peasant in French 19th Century Art* (Dublin: The Douglas Hyde Gallery, Trinity College, 1980).

In the present essay, I am limiting myself to a survey of images relating to the Eastern farm, rather than the frontier. See Patricia Hills, *The American Frontier: Images and Myths* (New York: Whitney Museum of American Art, 1973).

I want to thank Kevin Whitfield, Bettye Pruitt, and Albert Boime for reading earlier drafts of the manuscript and for their suggestions. I am also grateful to the Charles Warren Center for Studies in American History, Harvard University, where I was a fellow in 1982-83 and where I did much of the research.

1. Although most historians stress the communitarian character of preindustrial farming, some, such as James T. Lemon, have stressed the entrepreneurial characteristics. The arguments are reviewed by James A. Henretta in "Families and Farms: *Mentalité* in Pre-Industrial America," *William and Mary Quarterly*, 3rd ser., 35 (January 1978):3-32. Henretta concludes, p. 32: "Most men, women and children in this yeoman society continued to view the world through the prism of family values. This cultural outlook—this inbred pattern of behavior—set certain limits on personal autonomy, entrepreneurial activity, religious membership, and even political imagery." [Henretta seems to imply that family values come into conflict with entrepreneurial values.]

2. See Chapter VI, "The Progress of Farm Mechanization," in Fred A. Shannon, *The Farmer's Last Frontier: Agriculture, 1860-1897*, vol. 5, *The Economic History of the United States* (New York: Farrar Rinehart, Inc., 1945).

3. "The National Academy of Design", *The Crayon* 5 (June 1859):189.

4. Asher B. Durand, "Letters on Landscape Painting. Letter IV," *The Crayon* 7 (14 February 1855):98. Durand could well have had in mind Lumen Reed, a self-made, wealthy wholesale grocer who bought pictures from Durand, Thomas Cole, and William Sidney Mount. That very entrepreneurial energy which boosted Reed economically also catapulted him into the ranks of leading art patrons. That artists such as Durand shared common points of view with their patrons did not close them off from freely choosing themes outside this value system,

Fig. 56. Eastman Johnson, *The Cranberry Harvest, Island of Nantucket*, 1880, 27½ × 54⅝ in. The Putnam Foundation Collection, Timken Art Gallery, San Diego, California.

but influenced by market pressures (like men engaged in any other enterprise), they chose themes they knew would sell. Professor Alan Wallach is engaged in a comprehensive study of the influence of Thomas Cole's patronage on his art.

This passage was first brought to my attention by Professor Wayne Craven, who quoted from parts of the same "Letter," in a lecture he gave in November 1981 at a symposium at Northwestern University in which we both participated. The occasion was the exhibition *Life in 19th Century America*, curated by David M. Sokol, held at the Terra Museum of American Art, Evanston, Illinois (see the catalogue of same). Craven made much the same point regarding Durand, his patrons, and the market as I am making here for all of genre painting.

At the beginning of this "Letter," p. 97, Durand states, "We cannot serve God and mammon." Artists "whose ruling motive . . . is money" pervert art "to the servility of a mere trade." In other words, an artist's motive should not be money, but he must be made aware of how the patron finds pleasure in a painting. This double-think (whether sincere or cynical) has permeated the thinking and rhetoric of artists since art became Art, since its "ennoblement" in the Renaissance.

Durand's patron disposed "in his favorite arm-chair" reminds me of the often quoted passage from Henri Matisse, "Notes of a Painter" (1908), trans. Margaret Scolari Barr for Alfred H. Barr, Jr., *Henri-Matisse* (New York: The Museum of Modern Art, 1931), and anthologized in Herschel B. Chipp, *Theories of Modern Art* (Berkeley: University of California Press, 1968), p. 135: "What I dream of is an art of balance, of purity and serenity devoid of troubling or depressing subject matter, an art which might be for every mental worker, be he businessman or writer, like an appeasing influence, like a mental soother, something like a good armchair in which to rest from physical fatigue."

5. I use the term "Age of Laissez Nous Faire" as the historical period was described by William Appleman Williams, *The Contours of American History* (1961; Chicago: Quadrangle Books, 1966). Williams argues that the period of Laissez Nous Faire spanned 1819 to 1896 and was characterized by a "breaking away from the mercantilist conception of a corporate commonwealth," p. 228. The new breed of men "valued the liberty to get rich more than the opportunity to build a commonwealth. Hence they defined democracy far more in terms of unrestricted rights than in terms of corporate responsibilities," p. 230.

6. Richard R. Brettell and Caroline B. Brettell, *Painters and Peasants in the Nineteenth Century* (New York: Rizzoli International Publications, Inc., 1983), pp. 74-105, organize their survey of "The Peasant Image" into four "Bourgeois Values": work, family, religion, and patriotism. [See Griselda Pollock, "Revising or Reviving Realism?," *Art History* 7 (September 1984):359-68, for a critique of the Brettells' methodology.] It must be mentioned here that the Brettells' treatment of the American rural image is not only skimpy but misleading.

The association of the values I have outlined here with entrepreneurial enterprise continues to be assumed by many writers today (not necessarily historians, sociologists, or anthropologists). The headline for an article by Ellen Hume, Staff Reporter, in *The Wall Street Journal*, 21 March 1985, p. 1, reads: "Vietnam's Legacy / Indochinese Refugees / Adapt Quickly in U. S. / Using Survival Skills / Some Early Arrivals Make It / In Entrepreneurial Jobs; / Values That Spell Success / Work, School, Thrift, Family."

7. See, for example, Chapter VII, "Contemporary Views of Class," in Jackson Turner Main, *The Social Structure of Revolutionary America* (Princeton, N.J.: Princeton University Press, 1965).

8. J. Hector St. John de Crèvecoeur, *Letters from an American Farmer and Sketches of Eighteenth-Century America*, ed. with an Intro. by Albert E. Stone (New York: Penguin Books, 1981), p. 67. Also quoted in Henry Nash Smith, *Virgin Land: The American West as Symbol and Myth* (1950; Cambridge, Mass.: Harvard University Press, 1970), p. 127.

9. Smith, p. 135. See also Chapter I, "The Agrarian Myth and Commercial Realities," in Richard Hofstadter, *The Age of Reform: From Bryan to F. D. R.* (New York: Vintage Books, 1955). Hofstadter's definition of myth is relevant here: "By 'myth,' as I use the word here, I do not mean an idea that is simply false, but rather one that so effectively embodies men's values that it profoundly influences their way of perceiving reality and hence their behavior. In this sense myths may have vary-

ing degrees of fiction or reality. The agrarian myth became increasingly fictional as time went on," p. 24.

Regarding the realities, as revealed by the historian's statistical methods, see Clarence H. Danhof, *Change in Agriculture: The Northern United States, 1820-1870* (Cambridge, Mass.: Harvard University Press, 1969), pp. 73-129.

10. I make this claim fully cognizant of Pollock's assertion in her review "Revising or Reviving Realism?," p. 362, that: "Pictures cannot be carriers of value or anything else for that matter; they are systems of signs, as objects or as texts, which circulate amongst subjects who are both constituted by the act of viewing and reading and constitutive of a reading." The point she raises needs amplification. Were I to argue in what sense signs and systems can be said to be "carriers of value" the present essay would lengthen considerably. Certainly pictures functioned no differently in the culture than popular novels, etiquette books, manuals on home decorating, etc., in terms of their ability to create desires and thus to affect social behavior. The extent to which this actually happens is currently being debated by historians, psychologists, et al.

11. "American Painters: Their Errors as Regards Nationality," *Cosmopolitan Art Journal* 1, no. 4 (June 1857):116, quoted in Patricia Hills, *The Painters' America: Rural and Urban Life, 1810-1910* (New York: Praeger Publishers in Association with the Whitney Museum of American Art, 1974), p. 29, 34. Commercial factors certainly influenced this writer. The *Cosmopolitan Art Journal* was the organ of the Cosmopolitan Art Association which sold pictures and competed with the American Art-Union.

12. What differentiates American painting from nineteenth-century European painting is that it continued throughout most of the century to be optimistic and that a *critical realism* developed so late. Aside from a few satirists, such as David Gilmour Blythe, it was not until 1886 that any major painter exhibited a work critical of industrial capitalism, and that was Robert Koehler's *The Strike* (Collection Lee Baxandall, on loan to District 1199, New York City). Until then, no radical or revolutionary images found a place in the history of American art anywhere near the equal of Delacroix's *Liberty Leading the People* or Gericault's *Raft of the Medusa*. The reasons for the delay in social consciousness entering the mainstream of artistic themes are complex and beyond the scope of this essay, but it largely concerns the fact that radical and socialist movements developed slowly in the United States. For a survey of the urban or industrial worker in American painting, see Hills, "The Fine Arts in America: Images of Labor from 1800 to 1950," in Robert Weible, ed., *Essays from the Lowell Conference on Industrial History: 1982, The Arts and Industrialism; 1983, The Industrial City* (North Andover, Mass.: Museum of American Textile History, 1985), pp. 120-64.

13. To examine *why* these values were important to the entrepreneurial class gets to the heart of the concept of ideology, defined in modern times as the study of the relationships between ideas and material interests. See Raymond Williams, *Keywords: A Vocabulary of Culture and Society* (New York: Oxford University Press, 1976), pp. 126-30. Such an examination, because it would be controversial, would necessarily be vast, intricate, and deserving of thorough research and documentation. I suspect that such a study would point not just to the high value which our nineteenth-century ideologues placed on productivity but also to a general shift in the culture toward consumerism. For example, the concept of egalitarianism is not just political but also economic. It encourages the behavior pattern of "keeping up with the Joneses," which, as we know, brings people into the marketplace.

For reproductions of American genre paintings, see Hermann Warner Williams, Jr., *Mirror to the American Past: A Survey of American Genre Painting: 1750-1900* (Greenwich, Conn.: New York Graphic Society, 1973), and Joshua C. Taylor, *America as Art* (Washington, D.C.: Smithsonian Institution Press, 1976), as well as Hills, *The Painters' America*, and David M. Sokol, *Life in 19th Century America*, exhibition catalogue (Evanston, Ill.: Terra Museum of American Art, 1981).

14. *The Virginia Gazette and American Advertiser*, 21 December 1782, quoted in Main, *The Social Structure of Revolutionary America*, p. 262.

15. Duke de la Rochefoucault-Liancourt, *Travels Through the United States of North America*, 2 vols. (London, 1799), 2:215, quoted in Main, p. 254. Main concludes that Rochefoucault-Liancourt is a more reliable source than de Crèvecoeur, "who writes from his artistic imagination and is unreliable despite his reputation," p. 297.

16. My claim regarding the paucity of newspapers in European genre painting is based on a perusal of Gabriel P. Weisberg, *The Realist Tradition: French Painting and Drawing, 1830-1900* (Cleveland: The Cleveland Museum of Art, 1980), Brettell, and other standard texts. A more thorough investigation is still in order.

17. "Explanation of the Plates," *The Analectic Magazine*, n. s. 1, 1 (February 1820), p. 175, quoted in Hills, *The Painters' America*, pp. 2, 5.

18. The American Art-Union, an influential mid-century source of patronage for American artists, was founded as a non-profit organization by a number of businessmen in 1839. At first called the Apollo Association for the Promotion of the Fine Arts in the United States, its stated aims were "cultivating the talent of artists" and "promoting the popular taste." To this end, it bought paintings from American artists and distributed them by lottery to its subscribers. (In 1849, at its peak, it distributed 1,010 works of art among 18,960 subscribers.) In addition, it issued one or two engravings each year to all its members and published an illustrated periodical from April 1848 through December 1851. The American Art-Union folded in 1853, largely as the result of legal actions brought against it. See Charles E. Baker, "The American Art-Union," in Bartlett Cowdrey, *The American Academy of Fine Arts and American Art-Union*, 2 vols. (New York: The New-York Historical Society, 1953), 1:95-240. See also E. M. Bloch, "The American Art-Union's Downfall," *The New-York Historical Society Quarterly* 37 (1953):331-59; and Maybelle Mann, *The American Art-Union* (Otisville, N. Y.: ALM Associates, Inc., 1977).

19. Quoted in Alfred Frankenstein, *William Sidney Mount* (New York: Harry N. Abrams, Inc., 1975), p. 32. Frankenstein, p. 202, summarizes the interpretation given to this painting by a student of his, Joseph Hudson: "Mr. Hudson points out that in the campaign of 1852 the right-wing Democrats (Mount's faction) united with the right-wing Whigs to elect Franklin Pierce president. The politics of that year let down the bars between the parties, and Mount depicts himself reading a leading Whig newspaper." Elizabeth Johns has also been researching the political "punning" characteristic of Mount's work.

20. Alexis de Tocqueville, *Democracy in America*, 2 vols. (New York: Vintage Books, 1945), 1:180.

21. The peripheral status of blacks and women is discussed in Hills, *The Painters' America*, pp. 12, 16.

22. See Robert F. Westervelt, "The Whig Painter of Missouri," *The American Art Journal* 2, no. 1 (Spring 1970):46-53.

23. Krimmel did several earlier election day scenes engraved by Alexander Lawson; see Milo M. Naeve, *John Lewis Krimmel: An Artist in Federal America* (Newark, N.J.: University of Delaware Press, forthcoming in 1987). Other Bingham paintings with political themes, such as *Canvassing for a Vote* (1852, Nelson Gallery-Atkins Museum of Art, Kansas City) and *Stump Speaking* (1854, The Boatman's National Bank, St. Louis), carry no ironic bite, although *The Verdict of the People* (1855, The Boatman's National Bank, St. Louis) may be questionable on this score.

24. I discussed such images in a talk, "Black Emancipation: Images Promises, and Realities in American Genre Painting, 1865-1870," delivered at the College Art Association annual meetings, February 13, 1986.
   Michael Quick, "Homer in Virginia," *Los Angeles County Museum of Art Bulletin* 24 (1978), pp. 60-81, discusses six paintings of country blacks that Homer did during the 1870s. He focuses specifically on *The Cotton Pickers* (1876, Los Angeles County Museum of Art) and sees it as a landmark in the history of American art in terms of the presentation of the nobility of blacks. There are other contenders for this status, but Homer's painting is certainly a major work.

25. Quoted in Frankenstein, *William Sidney Mount*, p. 70.

26. The symbolism of Mayer's painting has been elaborated by Edward J. Nygren in *Of Time and Place: American Figurative Art from the Corcoran Gallery* (Washington, D.C.: Smithsonian Institution Traveling Exhibition Service and the Corcoran Gallery of Art, 1981), p. 38.

27. Reproduced in Sokol, *Life in 19th Century America*. Pictures of Yankee peddlers, that is, men specifically involved in selling, were very popular; see Hills, *The Painters' America*, for reproductions of Asher B. Durand, *The Peddler Displaying His Wares* (1836), Francis William Edmonds, *The Image Peddler* (1844), John Whetten Ehninger, *Yankee Peddler* (1853), and Thomas Waterman Wood, *The Yankee Peddler* (1872).

28. Enoch Wood Perry painted *The True American* (c. 1875, The Metropolitan Museum of Art), which depicts five adult males and one child sitting or lounging behind the rail of a porch. The painter cleverly obscured all of the faces by a newspaper, a shutter, or the picture frame itself. The title refers to the name of the newspaper. See reproduction in Williams, *Mirror to the American Past*, p. 200.

29. 31st Cong., 2nd sess., 1851, in *Congressional Globe*, Appendix, p. 137, quoted in Smith, *Virgin Land*, p. 171.

30. See Shannon, *The Farmer's Last Frontier*, pp. 51-75.

31. For Eastman Johnson, see John I. H. Baur, *Eastman Johnson, 1824-1906: An American Genre Painter* (Brooklyn: Institute of Arts and Science, 1940), and Hills, *Eastman Johnson* (New York: Clarkson N. Potter, 1972). For Winslow Homer, see Lloyd Goodrich, *Winslow Homer* (New York: The Macmillan Company, 1944); John Wilmerding, *Winslow Homer* (New York: Praeger Publishers, 1972); and Gordon Hendricks, *The Life and Work of Winslow Homer* (New York: Harry N. Abrams, Inc., 1979).

32. See Barbara Novak, *Nature and Culture: American Landscape and Painting, 1825-1875* (New York: Oxford University Press, 1980), pp. 157-65. *The Woodcutter* is reproduced in Hills, *Eastman Johnson*, p. 52.

33. For *Answering the Horn*, see J. Gray Sweeney, *American Painting* (Muskegon, Mich.: Muskegon Museum of Art, 1980), pp. 70-71, 113; for *Song of the Lark*, see Dennis R. Anderson, *Three Hundred Years of American Art in the Chrysler Museum* (Norfolk Vir.: Chrysler Museum at Norfolk, 1976), p. 121.

34. After 1880 expatriate Americans like Daniel Ridgway Knight, following the lead of their European contemporaries, produced paintings of comely peasant women. Robert Bezucha, in his lecture at Omaha, noted that there was also a shift in the imagery of European paintings. In the 1850s men work; by the 1880s women work or men and women work together.

35. Lizzie W. Champney, "The Summer Haunts of American Artists," *The Century Magazine* 30 (September 1885), p. 854, quoted in Hills, *Eastman Johnson*, p. 87, where I discuss Johnson's late farm pictures at length. I have similarly discussed them in "The Working American," in Abigail Booth Gerdts, *The Working American* (Washington, D.C.: Smithsonian Institution Traveling Exhibition Service and District 1199, National Union of Hospital and Health Care Employees, 1979).

36. William Walton, "Eastman Johnson, Painter," *Scribner's Magazine* 40 (1906):270-71, quoted in Hills, *Eastman Johnson*, p. 92, where I make the same points.

37. For a discussion of this shift, see Hills, *The Painters' America*, pp. 84-113.

38. For a survey of art activity in the 1890s, see Hills, *Turn-of-the-Century America: Paintings, Graphics, Photographs, 1890-1910* (New York: Whitney Museum of American Art, 1977). I discussed the shift from an art of moral content to an art of appearances or spectacle in Hills, *John Singer Sargent* (New York: Whitney Museum of American Art in association with Harry N. Abrams, Inc., 1986), pp. 33-39. On page 39, I quoted the writer Edmund Gosse describing Sargent: "Sargent . . . thought that the artist ought to know nothing whatever about the nature of the object before him . . . but should concentrate all his powers on a representation of its appearance."

Fig. 57. Solomon D. Butcher, *John Curry, Near West Union, Nebraska,* 1886. Nebraska State Historical Society.

Living the American Dream
The Photographing
of a Nebraska Settlement 1870-1910

by John E. Carter

O N the surface the suggestion of a relationship between American settlement photography and French ruralist painting seems absurd, and for that reason this paper may appear out of place. Yet, if one looks at the work of the ubiquitous itinerant photographers in the American West and French painters such as Jean-François Millet and Jules Breton, one sees a striking similarity not only in their choice of subject but also in their treatment of that subject.

Obvious questions arise if one is to argue that any similarity that occurs does so by other than mere chance. Inarguably, the gulf that separates the painters and photographers is a broad one. Geography alone is a formidable determinant to be reckoned with, not to mention language differences. Moreover, the training and experience of each artist was radically different. The French painters were formally trained, drawing on a long iconographic tradition shaped by entrenched artistic conventions. The photographers, on the other hand, were trained in loose apprenticeships and held few, if any, formal conventions.

The difference in medium must be considered as well. The painter had the flexibility to manipulate his subject, to control light and shadow, and to influence the emotion of the work by choice and application of color. This flexibility, coupled with the iconographic traditions and conventions mentioned above, freed the painter to become more allegorical in the interpretation of subject.

The photographer, on the other hand, was forced into the creation of a more literal image, for a camera collected all that was set before it and rendered the subject only in tone, not in colors. This, together with the absence of formal training, lead the photographer to develop an iconographic language all his or her own, shaped more by the popular tastes of the raucous, robust, unsophisticated world of the American West than by aesthetic conventions.

Of course, the common ground which the artists share is not that of training, language, or technology, but rather one of vision. Each appears to find nobility in the existence that they portray, seeing and expressing the virtue of living on and in harmony with the land.

This vision is more than bucolic reverie. It is, rather, an idea, born and nurtured in the minds of Enlightenment thinkers of the European continent, that blossomed in the New World. The *philosophes* of this period embraced the notion of the unity of the universe, and because they saw the laws of nature as coming from the same source as moral philosophy, they found utilitarian applications for its study.[1] If civilization could be brought into harmony with the laws of nature, the evils that affect civilization would be eliminated; and if that happened, people might find happiness and fulfillment in this life.

This was a powerful thought, for it suggested molding government and society in conformance with the laws of nature; and nowhere was the unity of men and women with nature more evident than in the agrarian life. It was an idea that a group of French thinkers, the Physiocrats, captured and made central to their philosophy. While primarily an economic philosophy (and one which came too late to take root in the Old World), physiocracy found special meaning in other venues, most notably in the fledgling United States of America.[2]

The rational naturalism of the Physiocrats profoundly

influenced the shapers of the American republic, including such seminal figures as Thomas Jefferson and Benjamin Franklin. It was in the enlightened minds of these men that the tenets of the American dream were born; and it was this dream, this consuming intellectual force, that propelled people into the Great American West in the second half of the nineteenth century. Let us examine that dream.

The American vision of society was not based upon an urban model. Cities were to be few and far between, existing on a much smaller scale than that into which they have ultimately evolved. They were to be primarily centers for commerce and transportation, supporting a greater agricultural community which would surround them. This greater rural community would be comprised of an educated, landed population. America would be a nation not of peasants, but rather of yeomen. In the Jeffersonian mind, focused by the French thinkers

mentioned earlier, rose the idea of a democracy based upon a society of educated men and women who live on and work the soil, sustained by the fruits of their own labor, unencumbered by debt and beholden to no one—a truly free people.[3]

This, then, was the American dream—the siren song that drew scores of erstwhile peasants thousands of miles to a land of foreign tongue and alien landscape, far from the deeply planted roots of family and place. The awesome weight of this idea is felt to this day. To see it one need only look to the agricultural political movements like the National Farmers Organization and the widely held belief in the sanctity of the family farm. In the 1980s the lines are being drawn between corporate farmers and family farmers. These lines, bitter and bloody, have grown not because the family farm is in some way more economical or technologically efficient, but rather because of the sense that dispossessing peo-

Fig. 58. Solomon D. Butcher, *"Using All the Land for Crops," Custer County,* 1888. Nebraska State Historical Society.

Fig. 59. Solomon D. Butcher, *Sylvester Rawding and Family, North of Sargent, Custer County, Nebraska,* 1886. Nebraska State Historical Society.

ple of their land is fundamentally evil. It is an argument that comes, then, not from the cold logic of economics, but from a deep-seated belief in what constitutes good and noble living.

"The Old World imagined the Enlightenment," says Henry Steele Commager, "and the New World realized it. The Old World invented it, formulated it, and agitated it; America absorbed it, reflected it, and institutionalized it."[4] In the Old World the idealized agrarian life could *only* be painted. Enlightened despots mused on physiocratic notions, but little of consequence was done to affect changes. The aristocracy was too entrenched, the church too rigid, and the class systems too stratified.

But in the New World, all things were possible. The voices of the American Enlightenment were also those that crafted the republic. Statesmen were politicians, politicians were statesmen. The nation that they built centered on this philosophy of the quest for happiness in a natural, agrarian world.

Small wonder, then, that Jefferson's Louisiana Purchase was parceled up and given away to anyone who wanted it. The Homestead Act of 1862 was the embodiment of Enlightened thinking.[5] It provided 160 acres of land to anyone who would occupy that land for five years and make improvements upon it. If the only way to attain happiness was to be landed, then a good government, ruling for the good of its people, could do no less.

Settlers who came west in the second half of the nineteenth century were the first to harvest the fruit of the Enlightened American dream. And because that dream was more than whimsical philosophy, it could be photographed—it was real!

Solomon D. Butcher, a photographer on the prairies of Nebraska, was one on whom the importance of that moment was not lost. In 1886 Butcher set out with the avowed purpose of recording what he accurately perceived as the very transitory state of settlement. It was this perception that separated him from the host of photographers working simultaneously in this region of the country. Unlike the others, he chose to photograph the event of settlement rather than the people who did the settling. Thus, he looked at the pioneer's house, the farm, and the land as more than a backdrop for portraits. His pictures eloquently chronicle the interaction of people and place.

The motivation for the undertaking of a project such as this was similar to that which motivated the settlers themselves. Butcher saw pioneering as the embodiment of that great national dream. He had tried homesteading himself but found it too much work for his leisurely constitution. This brush with pioneering did, however, reinforce his profound admiration for those who successfully met the challenges of the land.

What, then, do his pictures show us? We see solid, stoic people posed formally, sometimes uncomfortably, in front of their dwellings. It has been argued that these tight-lipped, humorless images reflect either the strain of maintaining a pose for the duration of the exposure, or that life was so difficult and cruel it permanently etched misery into the faces of the people. Neither argument has any particular validity. Shutter speeds at that time were not sufficient to freeze the motion of a bullet, but they were adequate to capture modest movement. Besides, the notion that you can hold a sober face easier than a cheerful one is itself somewhat ridiculous.

Life was no doubt hard, particularly when viewed through twentieth-century eyes, but it was far from joyless. Jules Haumont, a Belgian pioneer in Custer County, Nebraska, who had himself succumbed to the seductive information sent out by the United States government, recalled:

> We came here to this beautiful country, in those early days, young, strong, healthy, filled with hope, energy and ambi-

Fig. 60. Solomon D. Butcher, *Peter M. Barnes, Near Clear Creek, Custer County, Nebraska,* 1887. Nebraska State Historical Society.

Fig. 61. Solomon D. Butcher, *Miss Alice Butcher on T. J. Butcher Place on Middle Loup, West Union.* Nebraska State Historical Society.

tion. Poor, it is true, Oh! how poor in worldly goods, but rich beyond dreams, in everything that makes life worthwhile. I do not know how large a bank account, some of the old settlers may have today, I do not care, they will never be as rich as I felt when I first settled on my homestead. I remember the time I did not have the money to buy a postage stamp. I remember the hard winter, the drought of 1894. The many obstacles to overcome. We came to win the battle, and we did. To what amounted those inconveniences, compared to the joy we felt when we turned the first long furrows of virgin sod, or planted our first fruit trees. We were empire builders. The future was ours. . . . [The] adverse conditions did not last long. No time at all compared with the long years of difficulties endured by the settlers of Kentucky and Ohio. Do not believe for a moment that, except for a few months during the winter of 1880-81, our lives were without sunshine and real enjoyment.[6]

Haumont certainly paints a picture of life different from that seen by those who argue the rugged-pioneer interpretation of Butcher's work. This is, of course, not to deny the difficulties endured by the homesteaders. Homesteading was risky business. Of the thousands who took homesteads in the 1870s and 1880s, scarcely one-third completed the term of residency required to "prove up" on their claims. Those that Butcher photographed, then, may well have had a hard go of it, but they were the victorious one-third.

Butcher's subjects are postured not as the tired and work worn, but rather as the proud possessors of the future. One can see this subtle but very real difference when Butcher's photographs are compared with those of his contemporary and fellow documentary photographer, Jacob Riis. The urban settings of Riis's photographs picture an immigrant population that is captive and defeated. Interestingly, both photographers had the self-avowed purpose of documenting and presenting a way of life: Butcher for his history and Riis to illustrate stereopticon lectures on social reform. The contrast is

Fig. 62. Jacob A. Riis, *Italian Mother and Baby, Jersey Street, c. 1889.* The Jacob A. Riis Collection, Museum of the City of New York.

awesome. Riis's work can best be summarized by the title of his book *How the Other Half Lives.* Yet, in Butcher's photographs one can see the character of O. E. Rølvaag's protagonist, Per Hansa, who, in the epic novel *Giants in the Earth,* looked over his homestead on the vast prairie and exclaimed, "Good God!. . .This Kingdom is going to be *mine*!"[7]

Butcher's photographs, then, construct what amounts to visual paradox. On the one hand they are of a proud, even joyful people, if we are to believe Haumont, yet on the other, they picture a people who live a life of privation and hard work. But then these people are the recipients of Jefferson's inheritance. As Haumont notes, they may not be rich, but, by God, they are on land of their own. It is this very *idea* of the nobility of the landed existence that is pictured.

It is at this point that the thread which joins Breton and Millet with Butcher and the others becomes clear. It is this vision of life that they share: Enlightened and physiocratic. Without question it is manifested in different forms, for these artists observe from entirely different vantage points. The painters look from intellectual understanding, idealizing a life which they themselves do not, in fact, live. The photographers react in an unschooled, perhaps unverbalized, perception of the intrinsic goodness of hard work and union with the soil. It is this value that all the artists share, born from a common font, and it is this value that they collectively express.

The issue, then, is not one of the level of artistic achievement, self-consciousness, or, necessarily, conscious or deliberate interpretation. Rather, it is one of deep-seated, shared values, what Gaston Bachelard referred to in his benchmark work, *The Poetics of Space,* as poetic reverberation. The ideas and values mingle not in the world of causality—of the bowling pin falling at the impact of the ball.[8] They are not consciously fostered or taught. They are so much a part of the fabric of the society that they are autonomic and self-evident.

This notion of the resonance has a particular significance when attached to these photographers and painters, for it forms a cornerpost of an ontological approach to their act of picturing. A picture, regardless of medium, is about time and space. It is the act of consciously selecting the events of a moment and freezing them. These moments are significant by virtue of the fact that the creator of the picture selected a specific time and place to abstract out of an infinite number of possible times and places.

By inference we can presume that communication is at the heart of the picture maker's activity, and that this person chose to make a picture because it was the best, most efficient way to communicate the idea, value, or emotional reaction that the maker wished to share. Without straining logic, therefore, one can assign the intent of resonance to the painter and photographer, since it is the logical result of the act of picturing. Unless one sees the creation of images as trivially self-indulgent, one has to presume that the maker of pictures is expressing values or emotions to which that artist expects a response, and not just any response, but one consistent with the values held by the maker. The conclusion at which one arrives, then, is that the act of picturing is a deliberate act, the purpose of which is to excite the recipient of the communication to some other-than-normal state: to resonate to the artist's tuning fork.

What the ruralist painter and western photographer share, then, is a resonance, a poetic reverberation to an idea. And it is in this idea that we find the relevance of comparison of the French painter and the American photographer. For it is here that we find the profound meaning in all their collective works. A meaning which not only affected the way in which they worked, but also affects the way we understand and appreciate their work. For we, too, share in the reverberation that so stimulated them.

Even if we do not understand the complexities of the human experiences that created each respective work or the milieu of the subjects presented by the artists, we can, in the sense of poetic reading, share in the philosophical value system attested to in each work. In other words, our understanding of causality is not crucial to our knowledge of meaning. We all reverberate to the same sense of the goodness of rural life. We understand and know that goodness, whether or not we know that its origins are in the Enlightenment, or that it helped shape the American republic, or that it affected artists whose work reflects it. This knowledge shows us how the ideas and influences spread, but it is superfluous to our visceral understanding of the principles and, thus, our positive response to the pictures. Knowing this, we understand the French painter better by knowing the American photographer, and the American photographer better by knowing the French painter.

Notes

1. Henry Steele Commager, *Jefferson, Nationalism, and the Enlightenment* (New York: George Braziller, Inc., 1986).

2. Ibid., pp. 47-49.

3. In his *Notes on Virginia,* Jefferson summed it up, "Those who labor in the earth are the chosen people of God."

4. Commager, p. 3.

5. Jefferson himself had introduced legislation in Virginia to provide fifty acres of land to every landless male in that state, obviously the seed from which the Homestead Act grew.

6. Jules Haumont, "Pioneer Years in Custer County," *Nebraska History* 13 (October-December 1932):236, 237.

7. O. E. Rølvaag, *Giants in the Earth* (New York: A. L. Burt Co., 1927), p. 36.

8. Gaston Bachelard, *The Poetics of Space* (Boston: Beacon Press, 1969).

Contributors

Robert J. Bezucha, Professor of Social History at Amherst College, is the author of *Lyon Uprising of 1834: Social and Political Conflict in the July Monarchy* and editor of *Modern European Social History*.

John E. Carter, folklorist and Curator of Photography at the Nebraska State Historical Society, has worked on a number of Nebraska photography projects, including *Dreams and Dry Places* and *Of Dustbowl Descent,* and served as consultant for Nebraska Educational Television's program *Sandhills Album.* He is author of *Solomon D. Butcher: Photographing the American Dream,* a book on the work of the nineteenth-century Plains photographer.

Patricia Hills teaches Art History at Boston University, is a specialist in American painting and has authored a number of books and exhibitions on American art, including *The American Frontier: Images and Myths* and *The Painters' America: Rural and Urban Life. 1810-1910.* Her book and exhibition on *Eastman Johnson* has established her as the leading scholar on that important nineteenth-century artist; her most recent publications are *Alice Neel* and *John Singer Sargent.*

Susan J. Rosowski, Professor of English at the University of Nebraska-Lincoln, is a specialist in literature of the Great Plains as well as an authority on Willa Cather, on whom she has written numerous articles appearing in such journals as *Novel, Studies in American Literature,* and *Great Plains Quarterly.* She is author of the recently published book *The Voyage Perilous: Willa Cather's Romanticism,* a General Editor of the Nebraska Scholarly Edition of Willa Cather, and President of the Western Literature Association.

Hollister Sturges, Chief Curator at the Indianapolis Museum of art, former Curator of European Art at the Joslyn Art Museum, is a specialist in French painting. At Joslyn Art Museum he arranged the exhibition *Jules Breton and the French Rural Tradition* and wrote the major essay for the catalogue. He also organized the symposium *The Rural Vision: France and America in the Late Nineteenth Century* held in conjunction with the exhibition.

Gabriel P. Weisberg, Professor and Chair, Department of Art History at the University of Minnesota, has written extensively on nineteenth-century French painting. His books and exhibitions include *François Bonvin: His Life and Work, The Realist Tradition: French Painting and Drawings 1830-1900,* and *Art Nouveau Bing: The Paris Style 1900.* He served as consultant to *Jules Breton and the French Rural Tradition* and contributed an essay to the exhibition catalogue. His articles have appeared in numerous periodicals, including *The Art Bulletin, The Gazette des Beaux-Arts, Burlington Magazine,* and *The Art Journal.*

Index

Illustration figure numbers are shown in brackets.